New Vistas in Spirituality and Science

Gerry Moane

Copyright © Gerry Moane, 2015

First Published in Ireland, in 2015, in co-operation with
Choice Publishing, Drogheda, County Louth, Republic of Ireland.
www.choicepublishing.ie

ISBN: 978-1-911131-01-4

A CIP catalogue record for this book is available from
the National Library

DEDICATIONS

To Joan, the love of my life, my greatest moral tutor and friend, with all my love.

To Peter, our beloved son, who has always remained with us.

With love and gratitude to all our family, spouses and partners, especially: Dr. Geraldine Moane, Chair, Editorial Board; The members of the Editorial Board: Eamonn, Nateghe, Maureen, Sonya, Caroline, Jim, Fiona, David, John, Nicola; and our grandchildren Kate, Maeve, Conor, Jane, Gemma, Peter, Daniel, Elizabeth, Bernadette, our great grandchildren Maila and Sahra.

To our grandson Peter Moane, Research Assistant.

To Sonya Mulligan and her assistant Gemma Moane, for the design of the cover.

With great love and gratitude to Mother and Father who gave me life and faith, and love and opportunities; who, together with Nana, Grandma, and Granda created a home where I never doubted that I was deeply loved even if it was never said. With love to my sisters Sr. Maura and Irene who took such a great interest in the book.

With gratitude to my ancestors and the many generations of patriots who loved Ireland.

With gratitude to the authors who most influenced my book: Father Enda McDonagh, Patrick Masterson, Richard Kearney, Jonathan Sacks, Ken Wilber, Keith Ward, Thich Nhat Hanh, Iris Murdoch.

ACKNOWLEDGEMENTS and REGARDS:

To the many extraordinary people whom I got to know in my journey through life and who gave me an appreciation of how well-meaning are the great majority of people; also to the many authors, too numerous to mention who shaped my thinking over seven decades.

CONTENTS

The Background to This Book,
With an Overview of its Aims and Contents.

Introduction

This book is, first and last, about spirituality. A Catholic all my life, adolescence brought reservations about some Catholic teachings. These problems grew as I explored various spiritualities. The ultimate outcome was that my faith in God and Jesus was strengthened. The book is written from that point of view.

Since my last years as a boarder in St. Jarlath's College, Tuam, my interest in religions, spiritualities, philosophy, in almost anything to do with human life, has increased with time. The seven decades between then and now is the long-term background to the book.

The short-term background began in 2000 when I first became aware of words spoken by Pope John Paul 11 to pilgrims in 1998:

"One should not think that life begins after death only with the final judgment. Quite special conditions prevail after natural death. It concerns a transition phase in which the body dissolves and where the life of a mirror-image entity (the soul) begins. This entity is equipped with its own consciousness and its own will, so that humans exist, although they no longer possess a physical body."

The Pope's words had been preceded in 1997 by two senior Vatican spokesmen. According to Cardinal Mercier, a confidant of Pope John Paul II, with respect to reincarnation every Catholic may believe what suits him. Fr. Gino Concetti said in an interview: "The Church has decided not to forbid anymore a dialogue with the deceased on condition that these contacts are carried out with a serious religious or scientific purpose."

These statements resulted from four decades of scientific experimental research by a Vatican team. It was because of the scientific evidence from this research that the Vatican, in 1997 and 1998, publicly announced changes in its thinking on reincarnation and on trans-communication between our world and the Afterworld. Ch 5 gives a full account.

For those who are not aware of it, the new scientific information about the Afterworld will at first be startling and almost incredible. The book, however, shows in Ch 5 that it is beyond reasonable doubt that there is a real Afterworld where our loved ones enjoy a creative life. They no longer have a physical body, but many of them have the power to talk to us and to take on embodiment. As one whose thirtyeight-year career lay in engineering I can say that the Afterworld is a material reality i.e., it has energies which can register on modern sensitive instruments.

If properly grasped, this new convergence between spirituality and science, deepens the friendship between believers and God, Jesus, and our loved ones in the Afterworld. The result is a more creative commitment to our fellow humans in this world as we try to lessen suffering and bring joy into life.

I wish to make it clear that belief in an Afterlife does not compel a belief in any kind of God. Naturalists, however would have to expand the boundary they have set to Nature.

On the God Question I avoid any attempt to prove that God exists. No conclusive rational proof of God's existence has been accepted since the publication of Kant's great works in the 17th century.

The corollary: that the non-existence of God cannot be proved by reason has been obvious for millennia.

A number of great atheistic scientists of our own era have voiced it in simple terms. For Bertrand Russell our universe was just a brute fact; for quantum physicist Richard Feyman the emergence of real energy from nothing was a complete mystery, not a proof that God exists; E. O. Wilson, in his latest book The Future of Life 2012, is a definite naturalist, whereas in Consilience 1998, he wrote that he "leant towards Deism".

These are just four out of many. Such authentic beliefs cannot be rationally refuted. They must be empathetically examined and respected as Richard Kearney writes in his 2010 book Anatheism.

The main aim of this book is to present the currently available evidence for the reality of an Afterworld that overflows with creative energy, and is the destiny of all men and women of goodwill. Three chapters (Chs3-6) are allotted to this aim.

My Spiritual Roots

My past beliefs have a history of being continually pushed to where they are now: no big moment of enlightenment, just a slow unsteady evolution. My parents, who were normally-committed Roman Catholics of their era, had me baptised in the faith of their fathers and mothers. For this I have always been, and remain, extremely grateful.

My parents ensured that I got the benefits of an excellent secondary education. They also enabled me to qualify as a Mechanical and Electrical Engineer at UCD, at a time when, with a family of six, their resources were reduced due to World War 11.

During first-year Engineering at UCD my landlady's older son lent me his Sunday Times to read. It opened up a world of new ideas, concepts, and imagination to a boy who grew up in the thirties on a small farm in West Mayo, and who was a boarder, during World War 11, in a college which was staffed and managed by young priests.

These priests were former students of St. Jarlaths, leading students of their year, who had gone to Maynooth. About forty percent of my fellow students went on to study for the priesthood, in various colleges.

Adolescent Life

Dublin with its student life was exhilarating. The girls brought their own aura of enchantment, mystery and romance to the scene. Those were the years when, for almost all girls, their virginity was sacred before marriage. We knew nothing about the most vulnerable girls, from less well-off families, who were abandoned to many years of humiliation and abuse, and perhaps eventual exile, because of pregnancy.

There were also boys who were quite capable of finishing an engineering course, but who dropped out in first and second year. Apart from the chaplain, they had no counselling for their problems.

I enjoyed my four years in UCD but could be described as a dormant Catholic, during the first two years. Starting third year, a brief 'line' which I had with a girl during the few months before the long Summer recess, was renewed. We were quickly into serious mutual commitments. Fortunately for me she was goodness personified. My serious life had begun. We married three years later and our first of eight children arrived one year after that.

Adult Life

My first philosophical book, bought from the first paycheck, was Bertrand Russell's History of Western Philosophy1945. Slowly a trickle of books on the human condition began to accumulate: on spirituality and religions, philosophy, history, psychology, sociology etc.

I had left St Jarlath's with a clear picture of the good life for a Christian: a good spiritual life, a happy family life, good friends, with rest and leisure given to enjoying good English literature and poetry, and Greek and Latin classics in their original languages.

It looked idyllic. All I had to do was add on a reasonable time for golf, some dry-fly brown-trout fishing with old friends during the season (it had been a hobby of ours since we were twelve-year-olds), and a week-end chat over a few drinks.

Leave out the family and the fishing, and it bore a striking resemblance to the lives of the many Irish rural curates of that time. In the event I did enjoy re-reading Homer and Virgil – in excellent English translations.

It was a time when Ireland's population of rural curates was around its height. The typical rural curate did not see his financially comfortably post as that of a leisurely country gentleman. They were deeply committed to the spiritual welfare of their parishioners. In fact the great majority were deeply immersed in every aspect of parish life: Gaelic football, theatre, and so on. More than a few were renowned for their abilities in various aspects of Irish cultural life.

I was not too far into my renewed spiritual reading after marriage, when I realized that a reappraisal of my school-leaving idyll was needed. Now I learned that the task of a good lay Christian in this life was twofold: firstly a committed search for progress in the spiritual life, by prayer, reading, and practice -- in a disciplined and programmed way.

Secondly, by using the inspiration derived from religion, and the aptitudes bestowed by God, to benefit family and other dependents where there was a commitment of love. Next one should be concerned for an ever-widening circle -- friends, neighbours, country, and mankind at large. This mindset has refused to go away even if the door was often closed.

In the second half of the last century I continued to give what free time I could, to spiritually inspiring books. A selection of such books that have been most influential are listed in Booklist A at the end of this chapter. Other recommended books are listed in Booklist C at the end of the book.

Epiphanies and Oceanic Feelings

These, I regret, have passed me by. My most fertile ground for anything approaching an epiphany would be melodic songs, from the middle-brow category, well sung. Occasionally, listening to these would make the hairs stand up on the back of my neck. One other event produced the same feeling: that was when I first saw the original of Caravaggio's The Taking of Christ. Its recall still brings the same effect. Yet I have been to many galleries both before and since.

Oceanic feelings: Scenes suddenly arising while motoring on the continent, the most memorable being at the top of the St Bernard Pass, with my wife and two teenage sons. Looking south over Italy on a clear sunny day: the same tingling feeling. Then I wondered did this kind of oceanic feeling come, way back in the past, to a Neanderthal man or even to a Great Ape alpha male, leading his little band south.

It seems that a need to psycho-analyse these events, brings me back to terra firma immediately. One lasting influence was an ability to appreciate the depth of feeling which so many writers could recall from their experiences.

It wasn't always like that: I still see and recall with great pleasure, our English teacher reciting, and repeating his favourite passages, from Milton's Paradise Lost:

"Thick as autumnal leaves that strow the brooks
In Vallumbrosa, where th' Etrurian shades
High over-arch'd imbower." **Bk. i, I. I. to BK. i.**

The story tells us that God hurled Satan and his legions of warriors into "a dungeon horrible, on all sides round as one great furnace flamed". From there they journeyed downwards ending somewhere like Vallambrosa. At first they were enchanted by what they saw and many thought they would like to dwell on earth.

I can still quote from memory many passages from our wonderful book of poetry Flowers From Many Gardens (For Seniors), published by the Christian Brothers, and now out of print. Unfortunately I have lost my copy, and even E-bay have failed to help.

What happened to these mini-epiphanies? I allot the chief blame to the de rigueur strict logic of engineering hardware design; it over-invaded my brain at a time of maximum brain growth. In France they call this deformation professional. It seems that practically all professionals, who go through their basic training during the years 17-22, lose a significant part of their right brain to their logical left brain, be they scientists, accountants, solicitors, or doctors. Women professionals don't lose as much as men because they have more right brain to begin with.

I have little doubt that animals have animal epiphanies. The domestic dog is an advanced species in the manifestation of interspecies affection. There has recently been a TV series showing remarkable examples. One example was that of a man ingratiating himself to a fearsome band of hyenas at a cost of life-threatening injuries, but eventually achieving recognition as an admired leader of the group.

It seems that God added epiphanies as a creative ingredient in Life's thrust towards transcendence.

Working Life

Cost optimisation was an essential part of my responsibilities in my first job after graduating from UCD. After two years I moved to a manufacturing industry where I was more deeply involved in productivity. To gain further experience in that field I moved jobs five more times in the following sixteen years.

Retirement came after twenty-seven years as the first Director of the M.I.E. (Master of Industrial Engineering) course in UCD. That course enrolled only experienced graduate engineers, and was the first such course in Ireland.

The twenty-seven years were a very positive learning experience. Due to innovative work by a number of leading industrial psychologists, particularly in the USA, an eventual sea-change in progressive management theory was emerging. The traditional master-servant style of management was yielding to an empathetic co-worker style.

Driving this was the recognition that creativity was widespread at all levels in an organisation. Hence the importance of giving workers, at all levels in their organisation, the opportunity to use their creativity. Therein lay the road to higher productivity and satisfied workers.

The impact on industrial engineering was huge. Fortunately UCD's Psychology Department was well able to respond and provided a major input into the M.I.E. Course. The importance of this development will be revisited in Ch 3. The Commerce and Computer Science Departments also provided valuable inputs to the course.

Remarkable Changes In Human Awareness

In the following pages I am going to introduce some of the more remarkable of the new vistas in religions and spiritualities. Some of these will give room for thought to readers who have been unaware of them. The same new vistas will bring religious discomfort to others. That is something I would wish to avoid. To readers who feel discomfort I repeat my belief that everyone should make full use of whatever teachings and practices they find most helpful in increasing daily creative energy.

The Paranormal

From my youngest days I had what could be called a 'shallow interest' in the paranormal. I had never any kind of personal experience and felt I had no aptitude for tuning in to the paranormal. However, some of my friends, whose judgment I respected, did have fascinating experiences.

These experiences seemed to have no impact on religious beliefs, or on atheistic beliefs. They were interesting topics of conversation after a social dinner, giving the usual wits an opportunity for ribaldry with much laughter all around. I felt sure they were irrelevant to my life.

In 2010 I had the awakening mentioned earlier, when I studied Irreducible Mind by Edward F. Kelly et.

This is a large 800 page paperback, each densely written page 23x15 cm. It covers all paranormal manifestations known at the time.

The Afterlife

From this book and my investigative trawl of the internet, the most startling and significant finding was that, from the tenure of Paul VI throughout all successive Papal tenures the Papacy had a special experimental research centre investigating developments in trans-communication between persons who were still alive and those who had passed on to their afterlives.

As a result the Papacy had updated its views on reincarnation. It had also updated its views on trans-communication through mediums, provided the mediums had acceptable attitudes.

Soon afterwards the Papacy accepted the reality of instrumental trans-communication through the use of telephones, radios, television, and computers.

The above findings are elaborated in Ch 5. However common misunderstandings about reincarnation should be mentioned at this stage. Those who have studied this belief are fully aware that no one has ever re-incarnated looking as he/she looked in a previous life (Jesus is the sole exception and that for Christians only).

This is because re-incarnates are born to different parents, and may be of a different race, a different religion, and a different sex; yet they may show certain attributes and characteristics similar to what they had in a previous life. They may be unaware that they have re-incarnated, unless some unusual event brings them to such a realization.

A common belief held by believers who have studied this phenomenon, is that the mission of re-incarnates is to contribute to the advancement of our species in accordance with the re-incarnate's capabilities. By their work and suffering they gain for themselves a higher level of awareness and of divinity entering their next afterlife.

Reincarnation will not appeal to anyone who feels that they have already carried a sufficient burden of responsibility and distress in this life.

Why This Book Now?

There are two immediate reasons for writing this book. As mention above I have learned only in the last five years that new and remarkable kinds of human awareness have come to light, that are highly relevant to spiritual beliefs. Yet during the long, public, 'God Debate' which is still ongoing, these developments have been given scant attention, even though many personal life-stories have been told in the media. I felt that there was a need at this point in time to make more people aware of the new vistas in spirituality and science, thus giving them a possibility of enriching their spirituality. The second immediate reason: if this writer is to make any worthwhile contribution, it has to be a small book, and his time is running out.

There is a third reason. I had finished my personal memoirs which would be of little interest to anyone except me and my family. My family felt strongly that I should write a book setting out what I believe. They declared that they would look after publication, sales, and the nitty-gritty that goes with publication.

Spiritually Influential Books and Authors

As mentioned earlier, the books I have found most spiritually influential are given in Booklist A at the end of this chapter. The authors that have most influenced me are Enda McDonagh, Patrick Masterson and Richard Kearney. All three are Irish and world-renowned.

Enda McDonagh was Professor of Moral Theology 1958-1995 at University College Maynooth, and Chair of the Governing Body of the University of Cork from 1995-2007. He has authored fifteen books and co-authored fifteen others. He has been a professor at various universities in Europe and the US.

Patrick Masterson was Professor of Philosophy of Religion at University College Dublin, when he was elected President of the college for the 1983-1993 period. He then became Chancellor of the University of Europe at Florence for another ten years. On retirement he and his wife set up home in France, where he continues his writing.

Richard Kearney is Professor of Philosophy at Boston College and University College Dublin. He is a visiting professor at a number of universities in Europe and America.

Summary

My aims have been to write a book that will be:

1. Creative, coherent, and spiritually informative about the new spiritual thinking that has emerged within Christianity.
2. Informative about the new scientific information concerning the Paranormal and the Afterworld.
3. Spiritually uplifting for readers whether they are religiosts or naturalists.
4. Readable by the normally-educated person i.e., in language that is as simple as possible for a serious book.
5. Referenced throughout for those who wish to delve more deeply.

My overall aim is to inform as many people as possible of the new spiritual thinking that has emerged within Christianity. In particular I believe that the new thinking about the Afterlife, properly grasped, will inevitably prove, in the long run, to be a great unifying force for our species: a force which will drive us towards our destiny.

For more than four decades Ervin Laszlo has been the leading exponent of a Natural Universe which has evolved from a Natural Cosmic Consciousness – empty of any physical form – to our present Universe. His writings are entirely secular: they give no clue to any religious beliefs he may have.

He is fully aware of the forces that are opposed to any new thoughts about spirituality. He suggests one to two centuries before a tipping point is reached.

As far as I am aware, Keith Ward is the only prominent contemporary theologian who believes that a natural consciousness was the source which gave rise to the evolution of our universe. He is Regius Professor of Divinity Emeritus at the University of Oxford.

My hope is that Laszlo underestimates the new creative secular forces of spirituality: The Human Capacities movement, the global Psychological Health movement, the Flourishing movement and others. These new movements have been getting impressive financial backing from governments worldwide, and have already achieved practical progress in human development. They will be the subject matter of Chapter 10.

Booklist A – Spiritual Readings That Most Influenced This Book

1 McDonagh, Enda - GIFT AND CALL - 1975

2 McDonagh, Enda - DOING THE TRUTH -1979

3 McDonagh, Enda - THE MAKING OF DISCIPLES-1982

4 McDonagh, Enda - IMMERSED IN MYSTERY - 2006

5 Masterson, Patrick- THE SENSE OF CREATION - 2001

6 Masterson, Patrick - APPROACHING GOD - 2012

7 Kearney, Richard - THE GOD WHO MAY BE - 2000

8 Kearney, Kearney - ANATHEISM -2010

9 Sacks, Jonathan - THE GREAT PARTNERSHIP - 2012

10 Wilber, Ken - INTEGRAL SPIRITUALITY - 2006

11 Ward, Keith - WHY THERE ALMOST CERTAINLY IS A GOD - 2008

12 Ratzinger, Joeseph - TRUTH AND TOLERANCE - 2004

13 Thich Nhat Hanh - LIVING BUDDHA, LIVING CHRIST -1995

14 Murdoch, Iris - THE SOVEREIGNTY OF GOOD - 1970

15 Murdoch, Iris- METAPHYSICS AS A GUIDE TO MORALS - 1992

16 Frankl, Viktor E. -MAN'S SEARCH FOR ULTIMATE MEANING–2000

17 Fromm, Eric - THE ART OF LOVING - 1958

18 Planginga, Alvin - WHERE THE CONFLICT LIES - 2012

19 Gaffney, Maureen - FLOURISHING - 2011

20 O'Donohue, John - ANAM CARA - 2008

Symbolism of Front Cover:

The inverted cone shows enlightenment, i.e. Spiritual Awareness rising through seven selected stages or Worlds. It begins with the physical world and rises to the Realm of the Gaurdian Angels, which is the highest level of spiritual awareness. Higher still, the brightest red symbolises the Infinite Cosmic awareness of God.

The tip of the cone represents zero time, which is the instant of Creation or the Big Bang. Underneath are two rectangles. Immediately under the tip the larger rectangle represents the world of anti-spirituality. This is the human world of crime and excessive attachment to earthly pleasures. The small black rectangle at the bottom is the realm of the Fallen Angels where they plot their revenge on God.

The various Worlds and Realms will be further analysed at the beginning of the Prelude. A deeper discussion of the events of each stage will be discussed in the relevant chapter.

Prelude

Definitions, Terms, and Structure of the Book

1. Awareness: Means the same as 'consciousness' in many contexts. It is given preference in this book because it is more descriptive of emotional activity; can be applied to bacteria as well as human beings; is a more common everyday word. Everyday-woman is more likely to use the expressions 'aware' and 'well aware' rather than 'conscious of'.

A major theme of the book is that of a historical increase in spiritual awareness from the advent, c. 50,000 ago of our species: Modern Man or *Homo Sapiens.* This is symbolised on the front cover of the book. The tip of the inverted cone marks time zero, the instant of the Big Bang (BB) c.13.7 billion years ago (b.c.e). Spiritual awareness then begins to ascend historically through nine stages. The ninth state represents the level of Cosmic Consciousness. That is the highest level of divinity that a human being can reach.

The tenth level represents the cosmic awareness of the Guardian Angels. The brilliant red surround represents the infinite cosmic awareness of God.

Unfortunately where there is free will, awareness is a two-edged sword for humans: those who are spiritually inclined will try to follow the light, but those who are unduly attracted to earthly pleasures may find themselves on a path of darkness. The first rectangle represents this darkening of the spirit.

The small lowest rectangle is black: the realm of the fallen angels where they plot their revenge against God by seducing his beloved human children.

But all the ascending levels in the cone have some degree of darkness up to level six, which is the World of Cosmic Consciousness and the highest level of divinity that a human being can attain.

2. Interpretation and Hermeneutics

These words crop up commonly in writings which deal with historical themes such as philosophy, history and spirituality. Interpretation is what the normal layperson does when she or he makes a judgement on the likely meaning of the facts at hand.

The word 'Hermeneutic' is particularly used in scholarly writing. It implies a deep examination of the context of beliefs held in the past, such as the meaning of words at that time in the past. It takes account of the well-known fact that words change their meanings at an accelerating rate with the passage of time, or by translation.

Hermeneutists are aware of the known uncertainties in their final interpretation, and are also aware that there are unknown uncertainties as well. Clearly, scholarly hermeneutics is a task for professional experts; ideally teams of experts in different fields.

3. Phenomenology is a highly complex idea whose analysis will be postponed until Ch 7. where it is an important theme.

4. The Structure of the Book. This should be read in conjunction with the Contents Pages. It can be seen from the Contents pages that the structure follows the evolution of **The Nine Worlds of Spiritual Awareness** as represented on the front cover. A chapter is given to each **World.** Each chapter details the evolution of **Spiritual Awareness** within its particular world, showing the struggle of our species to achieve and maintain higher levels of enlightenment, its advances and frequent failures.

Each individual member of our species who wishes to advance must, to some degree, endure the same experience of successes and failures. The price of freedom is indeed eternal vigilance.

Summary
Part 1, Chapters 1 to 3, covers the first three stages of rising awareness, from the physical inorganic world to the normal world of human culture

PART 11, Chapters 4 to 6, covers The Supernormal World, with its further three stages of rising awareness.

PART 111, Chapter 9, discusses the Supernatural Realm which deals with trans-communication between God and humans. At this level various supernatural modes of awareness can arise.

Chapters 7 and 8, can be seen as a prelude to **Chapter 9.** They present brief historical summaries for those who feel that their familiarity with these areas may be inadequate.

Intermission 1. Everyday Creativity, follows Ch 2.
It should be read and will show that every-day creativity must be practised in any life which is to be continually flourishing.

Intermission 2, explores possibilities for redemption, and thereafter for further creative living in a process bringing higher levels of divinity and awareness. We can glean important information about these supernormal processes from the many reports of credible witnesses who have partly experienced these worlds.

PART 1
The Normal Human World

Chapter 1
The Physical Inorganic World

Introduction
This chapter does not deal with any of the new vistas in religion, spirituality, and science. Hence it will be a brief condensed chapter. Readers who are new to this material and who do not wish to familiarise themselves with it need not read this chapter.

For those who wish for more information, the following references are provided. An excellent popular paperback by L.Krauss *A Universe from Nothing* 2012, is recommended as a first read.

The aim of the chapter is to list the extraordinary breakthroughs that scientists have achieved within the constraints of the prevailing laws of science.

It will cover only the period from the 19th century to the present, a period when radical social changes occurred which dramatically affected the quality of life of everyone around the world.

The Industrial Revolution
C.1800 The Industrial Revolution and Science took off. Cosmology and geology had already questioned the *duration* of the Genesis story. Evolution posed a new question. How could a benign God create a wantonly cruel universe? One answer was humanism, now atheistic and with a creed of human solidarity. It has become a strong world movement.

Cosmology: Until 1925 it was a given that ours was a one galaxy universe of static size. 1915 saw Albert Einstein's theory of general relativity (GR). In 1925 Edwin Hubble, by observing receding Cephid stars, found an expanding universe and began to map it.

1927 Fr. Georges Lemaitre solved Einstein's GR equation. In 1930 he, the first to do so, posited creation as expanding with a Big Bang from an infinitesimal point.

1972 Peter Higgs and others theorized the Higgs field – a 'vacuum' *filled with dark energy'**.

In the following decades better methods brought better data on distances and on mass/energies. By the 1990s Type 1a Supernovas (exploding stars) were giving much more accurate data than Cephids, and lensing techniques were yielding excellent data on measuring the mass/energies of Superclusters of galaxies. Lensing was based on Einstein's prediction from GR that large masses would cause light to bend as it by-passed them with the amount of bending related to the amount of mass. Also, an intervening galaxy magnifies a galaxy on its far side, making the more distant galaxy observable.

Finally 2001-12 satellite probes **(WMAP) 1.5 miles from earth**, imaged the whole sky, getting clear data on the surface of the universe 300,000 years ATB. It confirmed total *mass/energies* at c. 5% for visible matter, 24% for dark matter*, and 71% for dark energy. This gave the total of all + and – energies as zero, a feature of what scientists call a 'flat' universe. Data also showed that the temperature of radiation from the surface at 300,000 years ago had stayed evenly distributed across the universe as it cooled to present temperatures.

(*Dark matter exists between the galaxies in every
Supercluster of galaxies. It is estimated by subtracting
the visible matter from the total matter in clusters.
Dark energy is the total mass/energy needed for a
'flat' universe minus the grand total of cluster matter.)

Quantum Mechanics and Quantum Jitters 1912-2012:
1912-27 Quantum mechanics equations were completed.

1930s experiments showed that electrons could be particles or be waves; moved in discrete jumps; and could reverse the direction of time. They also showed that their actions were influenced by observation.

By 1949 it was known that all particles have anti-particles i.e. with an opposite + or - charge; also **virtual particles (vps)** were theorized. These could carry almost infinite energy provided they died instantly. Richard Feyman's equation, applying both GR and VPS, predicted subatomic data which agreed with observed data at the level of c. 1 in 1b. "Virtual particles therefore exist".

1997 Nicholas Gisin showed particles from the same origin impacting one another, yet 11km apart i.e. these particles were entangled.

A New Creation Story.
In 1999 Alan Guth envisioned the instant of the BB as a Higgs field vacuum which was a "boiling, brew of virtual particles and fluctuating fields." If stability happened for an instant, its temperature would drop; with the release of pressure an immense negative pressure could inflate the universe by a factor of 10p30 in 10p-35 seconds. Uniform temperatures would be created, with a uniform expansion and the properties of flatness.

Guth's story of creation complied with all the laws of physics; with the details of the universe's surface 300,000 years ATB; and with its ensuing evolution.

The basic beliefs of the naturalist creation story are:
1. Our universe self-generated 13.72 bya.
2. There is no God. We humans create moral beliefs.
3. We must all, with solidarity, embrace the challenge. Rx

Epilogue

Krauss's excellent introduction to cosmology was heavily criticised by philosophers because it failed to live up to its title. The text claimed that the widely accepted inflation theory showed that the universe could have self-generated from a quantum jitter. There are two problems with this. First of all a quantum jitter is clearly not nothing, it is a quantum of energy, and Krauss does not give any clear explanation of how it arose.

Secondly, there was no experimental proof of the inflation theory; it had not passed the stage of a reasonable hypothesis – the most reasonable one around.

There was a third more fundamental criticism. The idea that a material entity could self-generate from absolute nothingness was incoherent.

For a book which was hailed by prominent scientists as a lethal blow to the God delusion to meet such weighty philosophical criticism was highly embarrassing. The fact that it had been written by a leading scientist who would have sought critiques from his peers prior to publication, made the book's failure to live up to its title even more embarrassing.

Some way of recovering lost prestige was urgent. The way chosen was experimental proof of the inflation hypothesis. Alan Guth himself believed that with the very recent advances in technology experimental proof of the inflation was possible. He was selected to head the project.

Work began and promising data eventually resulted. Optimistic press conferences were held to announce progress which continued for some time. Then problems arose as the specially built telescopes got closer to zero time. In Spring 1915 a final press conference was held. It was announced that the technological costs of overcoming the extraordinary high temperatures would not be justified.

The project of getting experimental proof of the inflation theory was abandoned indefinitely.

CHAPTER 2
THE PRE-HUMAN ORGANIC WORLD

The History of Evolution

For its first 2,500 million years LIFE generated only viruses and bacteria. The bacteria gradually transformed the surface of the earth and its immediate environment, making it fit for more complex manifestations of LIFE.

As an aggregated mass, bacteria still constitute the greater part of living matter on our planet. Yet they remain much as they have always been: relatively simple single cells with a rigid outer wall and comparatively little to see inside. They are classified as prokaryotes. Yet these prokaryotes are extremely complex when compared with similar sized aggregates of inorganic matter. Laboratory efforts to create them from inorganic matter have not yet succeeded.

Eukaryotes

The emergence of a new and vastly more complex single cell is dated to around 2,000 MYA (million years ago). Current DNA-sequence research indicates that it arose on our planet on just one occasion. The descendants of this one cell went on to create all the known manifestations of complex life: fungi, fish, reptiles, plants and animals, including ourselves.

It is our common ancestor.

Eukaryotes have a porous outer wall within which there are such things as a nucleus, organelles, internal membrane systems, and other entities. They also have complex biochemical processes and programmes. Crucially, they have a capacity for the cooperative absorption of other cells, a key factor in the creation of new and more complex multicultural life forms. This makes their history very different from that of bacteria.

For some 4,000 million years bacteria have changed their environment with little change to themselves. Eukaryotes, on the other hand, created multicellular clusters 700 million years after they themselves were created, that is around 2,000 MYA.

Soft-bodied multicellular animal life was created by 700-600 MYA, followed by hard skeleton sea life (550 MYA), fresh-water life and first land plants (440 MYA), a range of insects, fish and amphibians (400-360 MYA), primitive reptiles 360-280m.y.a., a great diversity of reptiles (280-250 MYA), and the first true mammals to nourish their young 200 (MYA).

From the first multicellular animal life (700-600 MYA) LIFE's creativity accelerated through the aeons both in complexity and diversity, with interruptions caused by natural disasters. These disasters resulted in species extinctions some of which were massive, e.g the dinosaurs. In all cases however they were followed by rapid recoveries of the thrust towards more diverse and more complex life-forms.

Following such disasters only eukaryotic organisms evolved in complexity. Throughout all these upheavals bacteria have remained simple prokaryotic cells.

The Evolution of Humans

Primates first lived some 20 MYA, the common ancestor of chimpanzees and humans about 7 MYA. From that ancestor, one line led to the contemporary chimpanzee species. A second line led, through a series of hominins, to our species, *homo sapiens,* who emerged some 200,000 years ago in Africa.

Over the same seven million odd years a number of hominin species evolved in various parts of the world. At times more than one such species existed. All became extinct.

Fossil discoveries place the appearance, in Kenya, of hominins capable of walking upright at about 4 MYA. There is evidence that around 2 MYA a species, *Homo habilis*, that was recognizably like ourselves, lived in northern Kenya. Their brains sizes were 600 cubic cms – double the brain size of apes. It is thought that these were the first hominins to use fire for cooking. Over the next 0.3 million years *Homo* brain sizes ballooned to nine hundred cubic cms in early *Homo erectus* who habitually walked upright. Brain size eventually reached modern sizes of c. 1350 around100,000 years ago..

The archaeological evidence suggests that the initial take off in awareness began in one of the hominin species around 2.5m years ago: the first recognizable stone tools, simple sharp flakes chipped from parent "cores", are dated to that period and are seen as a first significant cognitive change.

It took a million years for the next significant technological change, the hand axe, to emerge: these were the first tools to conform to a mental template that existed in the toolmakers mind. Still another million years passed before the advent of a more sophisticated "prepared-core" technology.

There is no clear evidence of any further significant advance in technology, or in any other kind of symbolic behaviour, for another 0.4m years. At that stage two species, Neanderthal man and *homo sapiens,* had coexisted in the Levant for some 50,000 years.

The First Humans -- Modern *Homo Sapiens*

A new and dominant race of *homo sapiens* from Africa came to Europe around 50.000 years ago. Evidence from permanent European sites which were inhabited around 40,000 years ago indicate people who had "a fully formed and unprecedented modern sensibility in tools, art, music, burial rites highly organised living sites and sophisticated hunting and fishing techniques. The pattern of intermittent technological innovation was gone, replaced by constant refinement. Clearly, these people were *us.*" [*Scientific American* - Human Evolution – Summer 2003].

It is believed that language must have reached an advanced stage in such a culture. It remains a matter of speculation as to how and when human language evolved from the auditory and gesticulatory signals of our hominoid ancestors.

10,000 or so years after the arrival of *homo sapiens* in Europe the formerly ubiquitous Neanderthals were gone.

Recent DNA-sequence research has now led to the consensus that all living humans are descended from one female who lived in Africa around 150,000 years ago. No other human line managed to survive the climate changes and the many other hazards faced by our earliest ancestors.

The Evolutionary Chasm

Mentally, the evolutionary leap from the chimpanzee to the early Europeans and their contemporaries elsewhere, is unprecedented in the history of evolution. There are only two comparable leaps in the creativity of the LIFE process. The first is the emergence from mindless matter/energy to the first living bacterial forms. The second is the leap from simple bacterial cells to complex eukaryotic cells which occurred 2,500 million years later. Despite extensive biological research there is considerable debate among scientists about the nature of the transition steps which are assumed to have occurred in both cases.

There is substantially more scientific evidence available to underpin a consensus on how the more recent leaps in awareness may have evolved. Nevertheless, given the paucity of archaeological evidence and the limitations of current scientific knowledge, there can be no clear story of the mental evolution of our hominoid ancestors.

The Million Year Pause in Tool Development

One intriguing question is: why is there no evidence of tool development during the million years following the appearance of the hand-axe, even though brain size increased substantially? The archaeological evidence shows a new interest in ornaments and aesthetic goods i.e., a new kind of awareness. However the task of suggesting the reasons for this particular broadening of awareness falls to psychologists and will left to Ch 7., *Histories of God*. This chapter, like Ch 1., will confine itself to archaeology and the biological sciences.

What is clear is that 40,000 years ago, an immense gulf had opened up between our capabilities and that of our chimpanzee cousins, the species that is closest to us physically and psychologically. We were well on our way to becoming one unique world-wide species which would colonize, dominate, and transform our planet. We were also the first species to become aware that we are responsible for the welfare of all species on our planet.

Summary

Research continues to confirm the broad thrust of Darwin's theory of evolution:

1) among individuals in a population of any species there is variation in form, physiology, and behaviour;
2) offspring resemble their parents more than they resemble unrelated individuals;
3) in a given environment, some forms are more likely to survive and reproduce.
4) gene replication is not perfect, new heritable variation is constantly occurring through mutation.

While these basic principles are not in dispute, there is considerable disagreement as to why certain life-forms evolved, rather than others. The story of evolution remains a work in progress.

Bacteria occupy a special place in the history of evolution. These four thousand year survivalists have tremendous adaptive skills as a species, but have not significantly evolved. Given the history of our planet they are the best guarantors that life will survive future earthly catastrophes. If survival capability was the criterion of LIFE's value they would have to be considered its supreme achievement. Ch 3. will show that there are other values which humans believe are much more important.

Collaboration in Evolution

The once-off 'birth' of the first progenitor eukaryote is taken to be a collaborative event, a 'fateful encounter', between two bacteria. Thereafter phagocytises emerged. This is the engulfment of one cell by another followed by mutual collaboration within the larger unit. Eventually, by a similar process, multicellular organisms arose and grew in complexity over the aeons. The human organism is a system composed of a myriad cells of various kinds which are required to collaborate intensely in the most intricate manner if health is to be preserved.

Co-operative ecosystems which enable a number of species to live harmoniously together have always been a feature of the biological world. Only with the emergence of warm-blooded, mobile carnivores did predator-prey interactions become a leading, and an accelerating, feature of the evolutionary process. Unlike phagocytosis, such interactions mean sudden death for the prey organism.

Through mutation and natural selection prey organisms evolve who are more skilful at avoiding predators and in turn predators evolve who have the skills to surmount the new problems. Thus is initiated what evolutionists call an 'arms race'. Research has provided clear evidence to support the common sense conclusion that environments which are most hospitable to such an arms race, are also most congenial to the pace of evolution, and the development of awareness.

Homo sapiens, who in the course of 30,000 years successfully inhabited the whole earth was, and remains, the species with the greatest innate capacity for predation. Early humans also had the greatest innate capacity for cooperation, a capacity which, ironically, enabled them to excel as predators.

There is evidence, both from archaeological findings and from studies of actual hunter-gatherer cultures, that early humans were not thoughtless predators: they empathized with, and respected, the species which they hunted down as a source of food. Throughout our history these two capacities have continued to evolve. Today our survival as a species depends on our ability to establish cooperation as the dominant modus vivendi, not only amongst ourselves but also with other species,

A majority of scientists accept that the innate mental capacities of humans are limited, given that they have evolved from bacterial life-forms. What is surprising is that a mere 5 million years ago, after almost 4,000 million years of evolution, the highest level of animal intelligence was no more than that of contemporary chimpanzees, a species whose intelligence does not seem to have changed significantly since then.

Intermission 1:
An Essay on Everyday Creativity

"There is a divinity which shapes our end;
Rough-hew them how we will."
(William Shakespeare)

Forward

By the 1960s I had reached the conclusion that creativity was the ultimate driving force in our society. The great American psychologist, Abraham Maslow, had established his hierarchy of needs, and with it the principle that when a need is satisfied, a new need emerges until the highest need of *homo sapiens* is reached. He claimed that this highest need of our species is what he called peak experiences. These would be reached only by a few.

Like many people and societies around the globe, I believe that creativity is an essential need of every psychologically healthy person, that every society should be fully aware of this, and should take the necessary steps to shape itself accordingly.

I wrote the following essay in the 1960s as a secular essay.

What Does LIFE Tell Us?

Taking a broad view of LIFE's evolving history, its most obvious feature is its thrust towards more lives and richer lives: more as regards the number of both species and individuals, richer in the sense of species who have more complex organisms and a wider range of mental faculties. And when we look at the lives of individual organisms we see that each, in its own brief existence, strives for an enhanced life. It seems that, whatever its origins and vicissitudes, LIFE strives for more lives and richer quality of life.

Whether or not there was a purposeful act of creation, LIFE has a creative thrust by which all its creatures are seized, one which we humans have consciously made our own common purpose; this purpose is the promotion and enhancement of lives; in short it is creation in the most fundamental or primal sense.

LIFE manifests itself to us only in countless individual lives. Otherwise it is not accessible to our senses. Yet we know that its energy exists apart from the individual organisms that it creates; it enters an organism at conception, and it leaves at death. Each organism is unique; each is a one-off mini-process; it begins, it adds to and subtractions from LIFE's ongoing process, and it ceases. Each life, impelled by a mysterious energy, conducts its own particular search for wellbeing. When an organism engages in life-enhancing behaviour, which is its normal mode of activity, it is rewarded with feelings of joy. Ideally, each human life would be a joyful learning process whereby the capacity to select and follow the most life-enhancing paths would be optimally acquired.

In a primal sense, the words "life-enhancing" and "creative" have identical meanings and will henceforth be used interchangeably. For too long the latter word has been used almost entirely in an elitist context; the effect has been to exaggerate the relative importance of high culture and obscure the importance of creativity in everyday life.

Everyday Creativity
To clarify the importance of, and potential for, creativity in everyday life it is helpful to differentiate three broad arenas in which a person is active (or inactive) throughout his or her life and in which human activities can be life-enhancing or life-diminishing. These are one's personal life, interpersonal exchanges with others, and thirdly our physical and cultural environment. Activities aimed directly at authentic self-

development are creative; so is any interpersonal action or attitude, however slight, which enriches another life; likewise behaviour aimed at enhancing our cultural or physical environment, thus indirectly enhancing one or more human lives, is also creative.

Self-creation

The innate urge towards personal growth is most obvious in the healthy young child who spontaneously, joyfully, and unceasingly, exercises and expands his or her faculties. At an early age selected interests and lifestyle already reflect an intuitive effort to mesh genetic endowments with the opportunities presented by the environment. Progress brings joy, its lack frustrates, a truth which holds throughout life. Gradually self-absorption is complemented by an attraction to others. Benign nurturing and formal education aim at optimising innate talents and bonding instincts. Eventually a stage is reached where personal developmental decisions rest ultimately with the young adult. While the importance of self-cultivation has been realised, both intuitively and reflectively, in every human culture, Western societies have led the way in recognising the significance of individual differences for creativity in all three arenas of life. Never have the means for self-cultivation been so diverse and so widely available.

It is also clear that, given such availability of means, creativity in the pursuit of personal development is far from evenly distributed in our species. This is true not only as regards long-term choices, but also as regards the ability to seize the passing opportunities for creative pleasures. These may be sensuous, interpersonal, social, aesthetic, intellectual, spiritual; they will usually combine more than one of these dimensions. Such moments are essential as energising refreshment for the psyche and as occasions of thanksgiving for, and celebration of, the gift of life. They have special significance when shared with others.

Other-creation

The direct support of others in their efforts to live a full life defines the second arena of everyday creativity for the individual. Parenting, sibling relationships, teaching, the caring occupations, spring to mind. Long-term pair relationships and friendships offer their own special opportunities. The scope provided by work situations is immense. Recreational activities shared with others can celebrate interactive human play and raise energy levels. In fact all interpersonal exchanges, even the shortest and most random, offer possibilities, since anything which lifts the spirit of another enhances their life. It is a timeless part of our folk-wisdom that other-directed creativity not only benefits others but promotes one's own personal wellbeing and growth in a unique way. Here too LIFE has generously provided normal humans with an in-built urge. Again it is clear that, while all can beneficially cultivate this most precious human endowment, some are particularly gifted with innate interpersonal creativity.

Environment-creation

The environment is the third inescapable arena which each person experiences daily. It consists of not only our physical environment including other species, but also our complete cultural milieu: politics, commerce, science and technology, the arts and so on. Here too our species has inherited a sense of care for, and an aesthetic appreciation of, the natural environment and other species. And humans obviously have an innate urge to expand their cultural horizons. Outside the caring occupations, a person's employment is likely to be for a purpose (not necessarily benign) which is concerned with our environment - physical or cultural. Whether or not that is the case, in our private lives we all continuously interact, unintentionally or otherwise, with the milieu in which we live. The aware individual realises that any enhancement of a shared environment will benefit others in addition to bringing direct personal gratification.

Life Choices

To reflect on the three arenas in which we conduct our daily lives is to realise that they are irretrievably interconnected and feed into one another, that we have no escape from them, and that they offer inexhaustible opportunities for creative living as well as for its neglect or negation. A small selection of such opportunities, and a correspondingly vast exclusion, is enforced on each individual by limitations of personality, time, and material resources. The problems of choice between and within arenas make the selection of life-paths and life-styles complex in the extreme; in addition immediate contingencies incessantly present their own challenges. Complexity is accentuated by increased awareness which can both expand the range of choices and illuminate the claims of different possibilities.

By itself rational analysis would be overwhelmed. To a great extent we are compelled to feel our paths through life by trial and error, each of us aligning her or his limited and unique array of personal attributes and material resources to the inner and outer calls experienced. These calls are sometimes clear and inspirational, more often they are ambiguous, frequently they are both fortuitous and unwelcome. Decisions emerge, big and small, some provisional, others involving the most serious commitments. For the aware individual a sense of sustainable wellbeing is the guide. It seems that, just as the body has a homeostatic system which reacts to discomfort, so also has the mind a system which signals unresolved tensions and prompts a further search for greater harmony and equanimity.

This task is difficult for all, but more so for some, given that between one person and another there are variations in the strengths of the innate ego-drives and the bonding instinct. Nurturing in a reasonably benign environment allows the bonding instinct to develop and express itself; it also fosters the ability to forgo early personal gratification in the interests of more creative long term goals. These gifts are, however, relatively late additions to LIFE'S evolving repertoire of creature attributes. They complement, and can predominate over, but do not replace primal self-gratification instincts.

Innate variations also occur in attributes such as natural courage, adaptation abilities, evenness of temperament, intelligences of various kinds, charisma, energy, natural wisdom and imagination.

As well as genetic endowments and family nurturing experience, fortuitous events have their impact at all stages of life. Modern research indicates that the peer-group plays a major role in the character formation of the adolescent and young adult. Random experiences can also shape attitudes towards life Perceived threats to wellbeing can arouse and strengthen primitive self-survival reactions and establish negative mindsets, conscious and unconscious, which are difficult to erase. Even within a small circle of intimates problems are likely to arise. How much more pervasive are problem situations in the wider, fractured social environment of today, which so many see as threatening and unjust.

Conscious and unconscious mindsets which have their roots in negative past events distort LIFE's messages and reduce the freedom to hear them clearly and to act creatively. The primal self-centred drives are unruly and in our highly competitive and acquisitive western societies are kept nourished by powerful cultural forces. The human capacity for fantasy and self-deception seems limitless; self-creation plans can turn into self-furthering agendas which may ultimately become life-diminishing, other-creation intentions can degenerate into other-domination which is even more destructive. In addition, mistakes or mishaps can undermine courage and confidence. Thrown into a mode which is fearful and defensive, humans can be seized by a pervasive sense of personal helplessness. The local and international tragedies and failures which are continuously reported by the media, with little offsetting positive reportage, can augment this feeling. Awareness and imagination are two-edged; they can produce despair as well as hope.

The more the focus on defending and securing ego-needs, however essential they may be, the less likely is it that an expansive awareness will release creativity in any of life's arenas. Fortunately he normal human is not helpless with regard to personal limitations, whether these come from nature, nurture, or fortuitous life experiences. For the aware person creative self-cultivation can expand life-enhancing, and weaken life-diminishing, attributes; and the means of self-cultivation are readily to hand. Regrettably, among the plethora of self-help programmes on offer there are many which overemphasise a narcissistic self-development. Even more regrettable are the powerful influences exerted by a dominant commercialism whose sway depends on using every possible means at its disposal to promote our instinctual personal acquisitiveness. A culture driven by a self-engrossed possessive individualism is unlikely to give priority to the human attributes needed for a sustainable creativity across LIFE's three irretrievably interconnected arenas. The choice of an appropriate self-development program is a primary and essential step towards a creative life

Thus, while the creative urge is an obvious and pervasive feature of LIFE, most lives fall well short of their potential, even amongst those who are well endowed with human attributes, good nurturing, and a benign environment. In short, LIFE'S endowments are not all unambiguously benign; ego-drives, necessary as they are, can obscure our vision of the authentically creative and lead us along life-paths which may be ultimately destructive of well-being. The task for the individual is to harmonise the latter powerful drives with the urges towards creativity across all arenas of life.

Destiny and Freewill

Is there "a divinity which shapes our ends, rough-hew them how we will"? It is true that as young adults each one of us is already the product of two processes over which we had no control. The first is a unique inheritance of genes, the second is a unique nurturing history with all its fortuitous events. Furthermore, we each find ourselves in a particular situation, within an established cultural milieu, at a certain point in time. From these initial conditions, each of us charts a way in an environment which is subject to many unforeseen events, for example health itself is only partially controllable. The word "fate" could be applied to our unique initial conditions, or to the fortuitous events which thereafter impact on each life, or to the combination of these two influences. It is more creative to say that we find ourselves in a world which has a large random component but that LIFE has given each of us some capacity to conceive creative options and a vital if limited measure of free choice at the various decision points, big and small, which we meet.

Neither the choices we make nor the random events of our lives are predetermined by any mysterious controlling force beyond our ken. In a broad sense, however, each of us has an ideal path which beckons - that path is simply the most creative use of our particular abilities. We search for it by learning to tune in to, and follow, those of LIFE's messages which prompt us towards creative choices. Many of these messages come from the intuitive wisdom inherited by our species, other messages are articulations of fellow-travellers and guides, both past and present ; others come from our own particular milieu; finally there are the messages which come from a reading of one's own particular human and material resources. Because of the ambiguities of our evolutionary and nurturing inheritances, and because awareness and insight rarely come without sustained effort, the authentic hearing of LIFE's messages is not easy; to heed and respond creatively is even more difficult.

Do humans have 'freewill.' This remains a contentious issue in the various disciplines which study and research human behaviour. The dominant view seems to be that the normal human has a measure of practical freedom in decision-making and can, over a lifetime, increase his or her degree of freedom by developing positive habits; alternatively freedom can be lost through failure to deal adequately with negative habits which lead to one or more of the many addictions, from the trivial to the tragic, which beset contemporary humans.

Pessimism or Optimism

In today's media-saturated world we are made aware of the less benign side of LIFE to an extent that can encourage a de-energising pessimism. There are those who hold that hope is another human illusion, that our vaunted awareness repeatedly manifests itself in disasters of increasing enormity; that our hubris has already sounded the death-knell for most species on our planet including ourselves; that, as a recent slogan claims: "man is the virus, aids the cure". On the cosmic stage will our species ultimately be revealed as even worse than a "useless passion"? For the person who is able to face the full truth of the human situation are there any options other than to self-destruct or to endure stoically an unsought and tragic predicament?

Such a stance is logically tenable. But, even for many who voice its logic, it is emotionally untenable, as their lifestyles reveal. For better or for worse we have been endowed with an urge to live creatively, with a hope that seems eternal, with positive feedback from creative activity in LIFE's arenas, with attachments to others that impel us to make their hopes our own. A capacity for creative living rests ultimately on an instinctual faith and hope in LIFE and in the value of each unique life in particular, including one's own.

Every healthy organism is naturally seized by LIFE's energy which it nourishes through whatever means are found fruitful. We rightly cherish our sensitivity to the tragedies which pervade earthly existence; such sensitivity is a celebrated part of our humanity. But we balance it by an awareness of LIFE's joys and possibilities. We need to continually savour those joys so that we may refresh our instinctual energies, celebrate earthly LIFE, and feel grateful for its gifts. Relishing the sensuous, interpersonal, aesthetic, intellectual, and spiritual pleasures which are to hand, we should wish to remain on this earth, which is our natural home, as we consciously try to realise LIFE's (and our) creative purpose and transcend the limitations which prevent us from enjoying more creative lives, however transient and fraught with pain these lives maybe. (See Ward, K *God, Chance and Necessity* 1996)

We also need to cultivate in ourselves and others the fellowship feelings which sustain our common cosmic project. This energising fellowship must extend well beyond the circle of our intimates and embrace not only all our contemporaries but past and future generations. We can draw courage and inspiration from those in the past who, with all their limitations, have tried to advance human values, whether on an everyday basis or otherwise; we should be familiar with that story and be aware of our debt. All lives, past, present and to come, are woven together in LIFE's unfolding tapestry. Every earthly life ends but its repercussion on future lives continue. The hope that these repercussions will, on the whole, be positive has always enhanced individual lives and ennobled the human saga. Illusion or not, that is its justification. That is why a society should see as its first duty the imperative to nurture such hope together with the virtues necessary for its realisation. That is what education and culture should be about.

For most humans now and in the past, hope has raised the quality of their lives and fuelled human progress. Will it continue to be thus; or, given the unpredictability of human imagination and awareness, is it possible that a psychological famine could eradicate hope, creativity and even the life-urge itself? We already see omens of such possibilities in our most affluent societies. The antidote is a culture which promotes and sustains all the necessary belief systems and practices which are needed to underpin the most widespread expressions of creativity, especially those everyday expressions which are the leaven of human life across its three arenas.

The most satisfactory short definition of humans is that they are transcending creatures. Relishing creature joys we wish to remain on this earth which is our home and we consciously try to transcend the limitations which prevent us and our fellow creatures from enjoying more creative lives. We can also draw hope from past progress; in the evolutionary timescale it is only a few moments ago since our ancestors were sub-humans without speech. Obstacles ahead we must see as challenges to be overcome.

Remembering our evolutionary past we should be concerned but not too concerned at our own failures to follow the golden rule and we should be even more tolerant of the failures of others; humans still have a long way to go.

Both aesthetic and spiritual experiences are significant parts of the complex of signals which LIFE sends to humans. Aestheticism and spirituality that are life-enhancing bring, each in its own special way, a sense of LIFE's value which lifts the human spirit.

Both are mental but predominantly non-rational sensitivities. The first responds to presentations, natural and human, which expand our sense of beauty or deepen our awareness of the human condition. In one of its aspects authentically creative spirituality denotes sensitivity to the 'ineffable', to that which exists beyond any milieu that we can reach through our limited creaturely faculties; in its more common aspect it denotes sensitivity to moral obligations and to the demand that personal morality be cultivated in the pursuit of creative living. It has been claimed, more disputatiously, that great art can equally point to the ineffable and promote morality. While efforts have been made to articulate the essences of both categories of experiences, they are essentially personal.

A valued dimension of life, art in its many forms has been and remains a worldwide human phenomenon whose manifestations are unpredictable and indefinable. Not all expressions of the aesthetic uplift. When a leading contemporary artist paints a urinal, how can the viewer be uplifted?

Chapter 3
The Normal World of Human Culture

Introduction

This chapter will focus on the secular aspects of human cultural history. Many readers will be familiar with the content and hence it is optional reading. Only a brief outline will be presented.

It is widely recognised that spirituality had its roots in hominin society billions of years before we modern humans (*homo sapiens*) appeared. The four chapters which comprise Part 111 of the book will be devoted to human spiritual evolution.

A Brief Summary of The History of Human Cultural Evolution.

The following are the historical manifestations of human culture in ascending levels of sophistication and awareness: nomadic small group organisation, pair bonding, tribal culture, weaponry and war, agriculture, house crafts, dress, landscaping, industrial crafts, sport, music, dance, poetry and literature, drama, architecture, painting , religion and philosophy, community politics, local and government politics, political philosophy, higher education; sociological studies, surveys and application programmes.

The Evolution of Morality -- Early Developments

Bonding affection, empathy, self-sacrificing behaviour, and aesthetic sensitivity are not confined to the human species. At some point in the history of hominoid evolution these sensibilities began to assume a new conscious character which found social expression. Here fossil records and artefacts provide few clues. However it is generally thought that a gap in moral awareness opened up between our hominoid ancestors and other primates that paralleled, and possibly even predated tool-making, four billion years ago.

Southern European Cultures of 40,000 Years ago

A new and dominant race of *homo sapiens* from Africa came to Europe around that time. They "brought with them abundant evidence of a fully formed and unprecedented modern sensibility in tools, art, music, burial rites etc., highly organised living sites and sophisticated hunting and fishing. The pattern of intermittent technological innovation was replaced by constant refinement. 'Clearly, these people were *us*.' 10,000 or so years later the formerly ubiquitous Neanderthals were gone.

The Agricultural Revolution

These modern humans had a hunter-gatherer culture for another 10, 000 years. A BBC4 TV programme in August 2015 presented the latest archaeological evidence that a sophisticated town culture existed in the Mesolithic period. The inhabitants farmed the rich agricultural lands of the Fertile Crescent. This whole culture was wiped out in the glazier movement that divided the Mesolithic Period from the Paleolithic period.

Around 15,000 years ago agriculture resumed at an accelerated pace. Cropping and animal husbandry led to larger settled communities and increased population densities. This led to cities with their advanced technologies. The first organised states and empires emerged c. 3,000 B.C.E.

The First City States and Empires

Technological capabilities expanded in no area of human activity more than in warfare. As population densities increased in the more favoured regions of Eurasia from the Mediterranean to the Pacific, tribes pressed on one another and on city-based regimes. It was a question of conquer or be conquered.

Kingdoms and empires rose and fell by the quality of leadership, the sophistication of armaments, and the lethal skills of soldiers. The ruling elites were themselves soldiers. The successful lived in splendour through the sacrifices of their subjects; conquered leaders died, their surviving subjects frequently enslaved.

Great rulers underlined their power and status by constructing vast works, building lavish palaces, and patronising art. Civilization had arrived by the third millennium B.C.E. and it has continued to advance technologically, administratively, and aesthetically, up to the present day.

Roger Osborne's 2007 book, *Civilization,* gives an excellent account of the cultural changes that took place from the advent of modern humans (*homo sapiens*) 40,000 years ago, to the global market place of today.

The dominant picture that emerges is of a five million long era of imperialism, colonialism, the continuous devastation of wars, and the enormous miseries of the vast majority of humans. Osborne, in a secular vein, also covers the spiritual side in the evolution of awareness. His book ends on a pessimistic note, with serious misgivings that our current global governance can ever deliver universal wellbeing.

The Bible, 2007 by Karen Armstrong, a 277 page paperback, gives a good account of developments in Judaism and the Axial Age, while Robert Wright in his acclaimed 1994 book, *The Moral Animal*, tells how morality and spirituality evolved from the earliest times. These and other books will be discussed in Ch 7.

Further Developments in Human Cultural Evolution

The three books mentioned above were all published post 2000. It is interesting to note that none of them mention the new scientific information on the Afterworld that had been published since the 1980s.

Doctors had published observational reports on near-death experiences since the 1980s. In the media, discussions on reincarnation had escalated since the 1980s. The historic Vatican statements on reincarnation, and on instrumental trans-communication (ITC) had been issued in the late 1990s, years before the earliest of the above books was published. (Ref Ch 5.)

As of 2015, the same lack of interest by the media in matters of religion and spirituality, continues. This is a clear indication of the resistance of our Western societies to new religious and spiritual ideas.

PART 11
The Supernormal World

Chapter 4
The Paranormal World

Introduction

The Paranormal World is the first stage in what I will call *'The Supernormal'*, a term which is now in common use in the literature. I apply it to the contents of Chs 4. to Ch 6. (See Contents pages). It is distinguished from our normal world (Ch 1. and Ch 2.) by a dramatic change in human awareness. It is distinguished from the Supernatural Realm, Ch 8., by an infinite awareness in the latter.

The Paranormal World covers events such as Telepathy, clairvoyance (remote viewing), clairaudience, (remote sounds), psychokinesis and teleportation (the ability of mind alone to move matter), automatic writing in an unknown language, and precognition: none of these phenomena can be explained by the existing laws of science.

While only a tiny minority of humans are gifted to the extent that their gifts have practical uses, scientific experiments have shown that a majority of humans have some paranormal facility.

Dr. Chris Carter's book, *Science and Psychic Phenomena* 2007, *remains* a classic in this field. It is a 300 page paperback. Also acclaimed is Dr. Mario Beauregard's 2012 book, *Brain Wars,* which supports Carter's findings. *Irreducible Mind* 2010, written by E. F. Kelly et. al, and produced by Virginia State University, provides an exhaustive historical background to the field of Parapsychology.

The Paranormal: Acceptance, Rejection, Acceptance?

With the Paranormal we feel that we have moved into an esoteric world which does not conform to our normal human world. Yet at the end of the 19th century Paranormal events were being investigated by serious scientists. Early in the last century F. W. H. Myers established the Society for Psychic Research in England.

At that time 'Paranormal' was applied to what was then a common activity -- making contact through a medium with loved ones who had died. Many leading scientists were interested in finding a scientific explanation for such strange events which seemed to conflict with the known laws of science. A significant number of eminent scientists took part in these activities and publicly supported these events as real events. Most scientists agreed that they should be scientifically investigated.

However, powerful sections of the British Establishment, including the established Church of England, the Catholic Church, the conservative newspapers, and the Government, were determined to prevent what they saw as anti-establishment ideas, taking hold in the form of movements. The prominent scientists who supported scientific investigation of paranormal events were ridiculed in the conservative newspapers, and mediums were harassed by the police.

The most notorious case of police harassment was that of Helen Duncan, a very famous and highly respected medium. She came under police surveillance when, in two separate sittings, she predicted attacks on British warships. A sympathetic Admiralty official who was present at the first sitting contacted the Admiralty and was able to confirm that no report had been received. Some hours later the Admiralty got confirmation. Time checks showed that Duncan had actually predicted the attack.

Some weeks later a similar sequence of events confirmed her powers of prediction. D-day was approaching and National Security were deeply alarmed by Duncan's predictive abilities.

She had to be stopped, but it was the manner of stopping that created wide public outrage.

A naval officer employed by the Admiralty claimed that Helen Duncan was a fraudulent medium. After a fruitless raid on a séance a solution was planned. The police raided one of her séances and arrested Duncan. The judge set her request for bail at an impossible level. He also instructed the jury to find her guilty. She was sentenced to nine months in jail for fraud, denied the right to appeal, and sent to prison where she served six months.

On release she continued successfully with her mediumship. But in 1956, the police again raided one of her materialization séances where plasma issues from the medium. The police had information that if lights were put on suddenly, serious injury or death could occur to the medium. That was exactly what they did on this occasion. Helen Duncan was left unconscious and, according to a doctor who was called in, was in deep shock and likely to die if moved. She died five weeks later with large burns still on her body. Her case is discussed in this chapter because of the recorded legal evidence which validates both her unique powers to materialize plasma and her powers of prediction.

However, the British establishment interests were eventually successful in their aims. The great majority of scientists henceforth eschewed interest in the paranormal. Its practitioners were portrayed as disloyal citizens. Catholicism and other denominations issued their own prohibitions.

In the US negative reactions by the same establishment groups were equally successful in estranging respectable people from the paranormal; it was driven to the margins until the 1970s.

After World War 11, books favourable to the paranormal began to reappear. Again the establishments in religion, in science, and in the military-industrial-scientific complex became disturbed and galvanized into action.

Paul Kurtz, of Buffalo University, was editor of *The Humanist*, the bimonthly magazine of the American Humanist Association, He became the leading spokesman and activist of the establishment interests, and succeeded in establishing the Committee for the Scientific Investigation of Claims of the Paranormal (CSICOP) in 1976. Very quickly a number of its directors became alarmed at the lack of scientific objectivity in the attitude of *The Humanist* and felt compelled to retire. Soon afterwards the name of CSICOP newspaper was changed to the *Sceptical Inquirer*.

A long battle followed between scientists who were members or supporters of CSICOP and scientists who claimed experimental proof of paranormal energies. The first group claimed that the experiments carried out by the second group were flawed on grounds of both practical security measures and of statistical methodology. The second group made similar counter-claims against the supporters of CSICOP.

However CSICOP had not foreseen, nor had anyone else, that they were on the cusp of a third industrial revolution which was driven by computerisation and quantum mechanics. One of its effects was the acceleration of innovations in the sensitivity of new electronic instruments. These were capable of detecting subtle energies which were hitherto unknown. If these energies could move the indicators of instruments positioned hundred of miles away there had to be detectable energies involved. New vistas were opened up in science. It became clear to all scientists that the prevailing scientific laws were no longer adequate.

CSIOP had also underestimated the growth rate of teams of leading scientists who were determined to explore these new laws wherever they led. The conflict forced the pro-paranormal scientists to tighten up their experimental procedures in every way. Finally by 1996 very large numbers of replicated experiments had accumulated from a number of independent centres using the most highly specified procedures. Taken together they showed an overall paranormal effect whose probability of occurring by chance was extremely low. The populations tested in each experiment were chosen at random from the general population. Some of them would have close to zero psychic ability, others would have high psychic ability. Taking all experiments together, an analysis showed clearly that a majority of humans had some psychic ability.

For some years the leading anti-paranormal scientist was Ray Hyman, whose professional expertise in both psychology and magic was long established. In 1996 he wrote: "The case for psychic functioning seems better than it has ever been . . . . . I also have to admit that I do not have a ready explanation for these observed effects." Since then there have been no serious scientific efforts to disprove the findings. Further experiments since 1996 have confirmed the 1996 findings. Further details of the twenty year dispute follows.

Mario Beauregard in his 2012 book, *Brain Wars,* presents the results of controlled experiments carried out by Psychologist William Broad and his colleague Marian Schlitz at the Mind Science Foundation in San Antonio, Texas, over a period of thirty-seven years. In these experiments various physiological responses were measured. There were 655 session, with a control group of 153 people acting as senders, and 449 people or animals acting as receivers. A meta-analysis of these studies gave odds against chance of more than 100 trillion to one. In some cases the receivers were at remote distances from the senders.

"These studies support the view that people can respond unconsciously to distant mental influences. Other investigations indicate that people can influence at a distance living organisms, such as enzymes, bacteria, plants, mice, and dogs."

Micro-Psychokinesis (M-PK)

Dr. Helmut Schmidt, a world-renowned expert, was the first to use automated electronic testing in M-PK. For this purpose he developed a special random number generator with a theoretically unpredictable rate of radioactive decay, **"and so his experiments are essentially tests to see if human intention can influence random events at the quantum level."**

This allows replicated experiments to be collected at a number of centers in a short space of time, so that when deviation from chance is slight, the huge numbers of trials can produce significant results. By 1987 Dean Radin and Roger Nelson at Princeton University found 832 studies conducted by 68 different investigators between 1959 and 1987, all of whom used Schmidt's approach. Radin and Dean did a **"meta-analysis which showed odds against chance beyond a trillion to one"**.

Since then, the majority of RNG type studies have come from the Princeton Engineering Anomalies Research (PEAR) laboratory, founded by Robert Jahn in 1979. Jahn and his colleagues have taken all comers as subjects, unlike Schmidt who carefully selected and trained smaller numbers. This reduced the magnitude of the effect, but Schmidt's results were corroborated to a highly significant degree. Distances were varied in some of the PEAR studies. Distances of up to 1 k. showed no reduction in the effects.

It is clear that a majority of humans have PK abilities to some degree.

PK (macro-PK), Spectacular Laboratory Experiments

While M-PK is crucial for proving that paranormal energies are real, and that the majority of people have some ability in this field, the real practical interest is focused on psychic savants and the practical help they can deliver. This is especially the case in experimental Army Intelligence laboratories in Russia, the US and

China. Much of this work is classified security work, but in the case of the US, its Air force has been particularly forthcoming on its joint experiments with Pear. The US Airforce has published a 200 page report which can be downloaded by Googling USpychokinesis. An account of the more spectacular experiments is given in pages 56-82.

The report tells us that the very first US military-intelligence R&D programs on psi, PK and mind control were conducted as far back as the 1940s-50s:

"H. K. Puharich had an interest in clairvoyance and PK, and dabbled in theories for electronically and pharmaceutically enhancing and synthesizing psychic abilities. . . He was a recognised expert in hypnotism and microelectronics".   The report continues:

"PK phenomenon was also explored in the Remote Viewing program during its 22 years of operation. Remote viewing involves precognition and clairvoyance, and it allows a practitioner to acquire information irrespective of intervening time or distance. . . . Col. J. B. Alexander (USA ret.) credits professional aerospace engineer Jack Houck for "capturing PK phenomenon and transititioning it into an observable form". Houck (along with Alexander) held a number of PK sessions, whereby attendees are taught the PK induction process, and initiate their own PK events using various metal specimens (forks, spoons, etc.). Individuals were able to completely bend or contort their metal specimens with no physical force being applied whatsoever. Numerous government science advisors and senior military officials took part in and/or witnessed these events."

In the 1980s Robert Jahn (Dean Emeritus of the School of Engineering, Princeton) " . . . attended a meeting on the PK topic at the Naval Research Laboratory, and warned that foreign adversaries could exploit micro-PK or macro-PK to induce US military fighter pilots to lose control of their aircraft and crash."

Chinese Experiments

Meanwhile the Chinese continued to experiment and publicise with English translations:

"All of the Chinese experiments reported using gifted children and young adults, who possessed well-known extraordinary PK ability, to cause the teleportation of the various test specimens. In all the experimental cases that were reported, the test specimens that were reported were completely unaltered or unchanged from their initial state, even the insects were unaffected by being teleported. The experiments were well controlled, scientifically recorded, and the experimental results were always repeatable."

A number of interesting details were included in the Chinese report. A few which are of most interest to this book are given below:

"The Chinese papers are all extremely interesting and very well written, and they show photographs and schematic diagrams of the various experimental setups".

"The time required for the teleportation of test specimens through various barriers was any where from a fraction of a second to several minutes, and this was not dependent on the test specimen that was used, the sealed container that was used (or its barrier thickness), which experimental protocol was used, or which psychic was being used."

"Before and after "passing through the container wall/barrier, the test specimen and the container's wall/barrier are both complete solid objects".

The exchange of information between the US and China eventually led to a joint meeting of their top level Airforce personnel. Together they witnessed the extraordinary laboratory experiments described.

Police Interest in Psychics

Police Departments around the world have also been forthcoming. If you enjoy watching real-crime TV, and/or true-life documentaries, Google *Police and the Paranormal* for entertainment as well as information. It shows that the use of psychic geniuses as part of their crime-solving repertoire is now standard practice around the globe.

As the police themselves put it, crime cases would be solved in due course by traditional methods, but the time taken by teams of police have often been dramatically shortened with the information procured from psychics. This can bring real savings in public expenditure.

Dr. Dean Radom

Dr. Dean Radom, Chief Scientist at the Institute of Noetic Sciences (IONS) has held appointments at Princeton University and several Silicon Valley think tanks, including SRI international, where he worked on a classified program investigating phenomena for the US Government. In his 2013 paperback, *Supernormal,* he offers powerful evidence confirming that sometimes truth is much stranger, spookier, and more wonderful than fiction.

The Power of Premonitions

Dr. Larry Dossey is at the forefront of bringing scientific understanding to spirituality. Compelled by his own series of accurate premonitions about his patients, he wrote the *NewYork Times* bestseller *Healing Words* in 2009. In *The Power of Premonitions,* "Dossey takes readers through some of the most startling documented cases of premonitions."

Summary

A brief summary of the research in, and practical uses of, the Paranormal has been presented in this chapter. On the face of it Paranormal events provide no evidence that an Afterworld exists. Its effects seem very much a part of our Normal every-day world. Once again we see the impossibility of finding any clear division. We have already seen, in the case of Helen Duncan, that there is no clear division between the Paranormal world of awareness and the Afterworld. What we found was an intriguing overlap.

What are we to make of the fact that bacteria at a remote location can sense acute emotional discomfort in another living creature? Is it caused by a direct telepathic link, or is the World of Cosmic Consciousness involved in this particular transmission of information?

Here we meet a situation which will persist as higher worlds of spiritual awareness are examined: we have clear evidence that real paranormal energies of various kinds are at play, but we do not have a clear picture of the laws of physics and chemistry which must be operating in order to enable effects to be recorded. Neither have we any clear idea of the communication links between the three Supernormal worlds.

There is also persistent evidence of negative spiritual events at the paranormal level. This has been demonstrated repeatedly in the use of the Ouija board to talk to spirits. It will be discussed further in Ch 5.

Chapter 5
The Afterworld

Glendower: *I can call spirits from the vasty deep.*
Hotspur: *Why, so can I or so can any man;*
But will they come when you do call for them?
Shakespeare, ***King Henry1V, Part 11***

Introduction
This chapter will show that new scientific information has had a more dramatic impact on everyday concepts of the Afterworld than on the everyday concepts of any of the other six worlds of awareness.

There are a number of reasons for this. First of all, no factual information has been available until the scientific analysis of near-death experiences produced very strong arguments that people had temporarily visited the Afterworld, reported on their experience there, and were likely to be strongly affected for the rest of their lives. Secondly, Judaism and Christianity did little theological work on producing a picture of this all-important world that would cohere with the picture they laboriously produced of God.

The result was that poets and mystics, catered for the few who were both educated and seriously religious, while all sort of scary ideas circulated amongst the many.

The Afterworld in Medieval Times
The Summer 2015 BBC4 TV series *"The Medieval Mind"* showed that in medieval England human-like ghosts commonly walked

around, usually at night, and were taken very seriously. As they often scared respected citizens, investigations were carried out by the local authorities and reports were written up. These were duly discussed at the next assembly and if considered authentic a relevant decision giving the details were filed. These files are still held by local Councils and can be consulted by any interested party.

The quotation at the beginning of this chapter shows that by the 16th century, 'Enlightened' thinkers were trying to change traditional confidence in ghosts. 'Ghosts', however refused obdurately to be abolished. They were forced to go underground as fleeting shadowy figures and, as such, they are still respected by the majority of Christians. A new and very different enlightened view slowly began to take hold through the 19th and 20th century. It met with powerful establishment opposition.

There were *people,* however, in the Afterworld who had no intention of being suppressed and they held the winning cards. Eventually, as we will see, they used the new earthly sciences to establish a radically new view of the Afterlife. Their power was dramatically manifested in the 1990s by The Scole Experiments

The Scole Experiments 1992-1998
"We must tell you that the work at Scole was very important. The links that were made have already enabled inter-dimensional energies and wisdom to assist the changes to future earth consciousness. Therefore, this final session is to seal the doorway that has been created, and to end ALL communications – I repeat ALL communications."

These words were spoken in the last session of the experiment by the leader of the Afterworld team.

There were five hundred sittings of the Scole experiments from December 1992 to November 1998. "Soon the messages came in the form of voices which everyone in the room could hear. Many of the experimenters experienced physical touch. A large table was levitated. Then came the materialization of the people and objects."

The experiments began in Scole, a village in Norfolk, England. Over the six year period they were also conducted in the US, Ireland and Spain. In their 2013 book, *A Lawyer Presents the Evidence for the Afterlife,* Victor Zammit and his wife Wendy name some of the senior scientists and investigators who participated. Earlier in their book they name more than one hundred eminent scientists, drawn from many disciplines, who were involved in afterlife and paranormal investigations.

Overall, this paperback, in 251 pages from Chapters 1-32, presents the broadest and best account of its topic in any book that I have come across.

"For the open-minded sceptic the evidence collected over a period of six years with more than 500 sittings by the Scole experimenters is absolute. Many regard the Scole experiment as the greatest recent afterlife experiment in the Western World."

The above final message from our friends in the afterlife to us who dwell on Earth, goes a long way to answering Hotspurs sceptical question: Yes, they will come but **only on their own conditions i.e., if they are appropriately asked, if the answering environment is hospitable, and if they can help.** Additional evidence shows that if loved ones are also present, they will surely come.

The message also gives us vital insights into the level of awareness, or consciousness, of our friends and loved ones: Their general level of awareness is incomparably higher than ours; they live very active and creative lives aimed at our welfare, and they are the decision-makers when they are called.

The first two of these characteristics are extremely difficult to take fully on board. Even though deep down I am convinced, I still find myself relapsing into talking and writing as if they are no longer alive, less mind living the joyful and creative lives which they are living.

Vatican Research Into Trans-communication

"Friedrich, you are being watched. Little Friedel, can you hear me"

Friedrich Jurgensen was a popular and highly respected Swedish producer of films and documentaries for central European TV channels. In 1959 as he was playing back and editing tapes of bird-songs, he was startled to hear the voice of his own dead mother speaking the above words -- particularly the words "Little Friedel, can you hear me". Friedel was a special name which only she and he used.

Such was the emotional impact of the event that it changed his life: he started a personal research program and subsequently recorded thousands of voices from the Afterworld. In 1964 he published *Voices from the Universe,* followed in 1972 by another book: *Radio Contact With the Dead.*

As a filmmaker he did a documentary on Pope Paul V1 and they became friends. Paul V1 himself became interested in the spirit voices caught on tape and initiated an ITC research centre at the Vatican. As we will see, it is probable that the Vatican had already been interested for some years.

In 1967 Jurgensen's *Radio Contact With the Dead* was translated into German and Dr Konstantine Raudive, a Latvian psychologist, read it and became interested in ITC. In one of his recordings, he too heard the voice of his departed mother who used her usual nickname for him saying "Kostulit, this is your mother".

Friedrich Jorgensen died in 1987. While alive he developed a close friendship with Claude Thorntin, a fellow researcher in ITC. Jurgensen was noted to be psychically gifted himself, and on the day he died he sent a telepathic message to Thorntin indicating that during his funeral ceremony, he would try to manifest an image of himself on Thorntin's TV. Thorntin duly watched and recorded the funeral on TV. He was amazed to see Friedrich Jurgensen amongst the people attending the funeral.

These and other images of departed individuals, some of which were imprinted on the hard drives of computers, multiplied as other researchers increased in numbers. Samples can be seen by visiting www.worldITC.org.

Adolf Holmes

In 1979 *Phone Calls From the Dead* by Scott Rogo and Raymond Bayliss was published.

In 1994, over several weeks, five American ITC researchers received phone calls from Konstantin Raudive who had passed on. In each case the call mentioned previous calls. The five persons called were George Meek, Mary Macy, Sarah Estep, Walter Uphoft, Hans Heckanin.

A number of researchers began to question the phone contacts: might they be a hoax?

But then ITC researcher Adolf Holmes received a file on his computer in Germany giving details of the phonecalls. His computer was not connected to the Internet and the message simply appeared on the screen. The message said that other successful contacts had been made to China and Japan by phone and fax.

The calls continued. One two-way taped conversation between Raudive and Macy lasted 13 minutes.

Sonia Renaldi (www.ipati.org) leads the biggest ITC-Association in Brazil, with nearly 700 members in 2013. Recently announced new contacts via computers, answering machines, telephones and videos, have added to the numbers engaged in trans-communication.

Other developments under way in 2013 include individuals and groups producing specialized machines and methods for tuning an individual's brain system to the frequencies used by people in the Afterworld. The global number practicing ITC in 2015 would reach tens of thousands.

The Vatican research findings have accumulated from the term of Pope Paul V1, if not earlier, to the present. These findings and Vatican announcements, coupled with the numbers now involved in ITC, constitute overwhelming evidence of an Afterworld.

The results of the Scole experiments were known to a very wide circle of interests during the period of the Vatican's research programme. Inevitably there would have been participants who would ensure that the Vatican was fully informed.

Dr. Ernst Senkowski

Especially eminent in ITC research was Dr. Ernest Senkowski who recently passed on. He was a close friend of high-ranking Vatican personnel. In 2000 he wrote an inclusive critique on ITC. In 2011 he was awarded the first Honorary Nobel prize for 'afterlife and paranormal scientific investigation'. (None of the present 7 categories of Nobel Prizes was apt at that time).

The title of Senkowski's book is *Instrumental TransCommunication*. Chapter 12 of book and other short article by him can be accessed on www.worlditc.org

Because of interactions between the Afterworld and the world of Cosmic Consciousness, Ervin Laszlo also researched and published articles on ITC. In addition he has himself engaged in trans-communication on a number of occasions. One such sitting was in a darkened room in Grosseto, Italy, where a famous psychic, Marcello Baca had for forty years been hearing voices on his radio. Over the same period, Baca had regularly conducted "dialogues with the dead" sittings for people who wish to contact dead ones. Also at the sitting was Father Francois Brunet, a noted French researcher. Laszlo describes the event.

"Brunet, who sits immediately behind Baca, asks, "with whom am I speaking?" The voice discloses that is Fr. Ernest, a friend and associate of Fr. Brunet who died not long ago. Through the radio Fr. Brunet and Fr. Ernest talk for a while, and then Baca (who continues to touch the radio) says, "do you know who else is sitting here just behind me?" A different male voice answers, "Ervin." (He pronounces it as one does in Hungarian or German, with the "E" as in "extraordinary" and not as in "earth.") Baca asks, do you know who he is, and the voice answers, "e unhorse" (he is Hungarian). The voice than gives my family name (it is pronounced as Italians sometimes do: Lazlo, and not as Hungarians, with a soft "s" as Laszlo).

Baca places my hand on his, and his wife places her hand on mine. Baca tells me, "speak to them in Hungarian." I lean forward and do so. I say how happy I am to speak with the person, or persons, "on the other side." I ask, "who are you, and how many are you?" The answer that comes is indistinct but I can make it out: in Hungarian (a voice adds: "the Holy Spirit Knows all languages"): "we are all here" I ask, thinking of the fairly strenuous breathing that preceded the conversation, is it difficult for you to talk to me like this? A woman answers, quite clearly in Hungarian: we have some difficulties (or obstacles), but how is it for you, do you have obstacles too? I say, it was not easy for me to find this way of talking with you, but now that I could do it I am delighted".

As regards the emotional atmosphere, this description is, in general, typical of the accounts of other sittings that I have read. Laszlo, however was primarily present as a scientific investigator. A special team of independent investigators were present both within the room and outside, monitoring for the possibility of a hoax. The monitoring yielded nothing; neither did any other similarly monitored scientific experiments.

Experiments within the room make it clear that without Baca's presence the radio produced nothing. His psychic abilities were the essential factor.

The Role of Fr. Georges Lemaitre

In 1936 Fr. Georges Lemaitre was appointed a member of the Pontifical Academy of Science by Pope Pius X1, and became its President from 1960 to 1966, thereafter remaining in close contact with the Academy and with senior Vatican theologians.

This is the same Georges Lemaitre who was the first cosmologist to propose the Big Bang theory of our Universe's creation. (See Ch 2.). Lemaitre graduated in engineering at the Catholic University of Louvain. In 1914 World War 1 broke out and he volunteered and served as an artillery officer in the Belgian army.

The carnage of war changed his outlook on life, and when he returned to his studies he moved toward mathematics and graduated with the degree of Doctor of Sciences. Then, still influenced by his wartime experiences, he studied for the priesthood in the Archdiocese of Malines, and was ordained in 1923.

He studied mathematical astronomy at Cambridge in England, and at the Harvard College Observatory in the US. In 1925 he accepted a part-time lecturing position at Louvain, but continued to spend time at Harvard and at the Massachusetts Institute of Technology (MIT) in the US. He was awarded a PhD by MIT in

1927. Such was Lemaitre's dissertation that he was now widely recognised as a world-class scientist, receiving honours from a variety of sources.

It can be assumed that Lemaitre would have been a leading advisor to the Vatican even before 1936 and strongly influential in its decision to be at the leading edge of relevant scientific findings. The disastrous anti-modernist policies of previous Popes was reversed; it was now to take a leading role in scientific research into the Afterworld.

Reincarnation

Reincarnation and karma are a traditional part of the religious beliefs of Hinduism and Buddhism. Surveys have shown that a significant minority of 20-30% in Western cultures also believe in reincarnation. The scientific approach to the reality of reincarnation cannot be instrumental as there is no evidence of the use of instruments in reincarnation cases

The approach must be based on the principle that if facts can be found which validate one case, then reincarnation is a material reality. If hundreds of cases across many countries can be so validated then reincarnation is a serious reality which affects how each of us sees his role in achieving the destiny of our species.

Dr. Ian Stevenson was Professor of Psychiatry at the University of Virginia Medical School and was also honoured as the Carlson Professor of Psychiatry at that institution. He spent forty years investigating children who claimed that they remembered past lives. In 1978 the University Press of Virginia published his findings in two volumes -- a total of 4,000 pages. It is still in print.

Renowned for his integrity, his publications sparked a huge interest in the USA where polls showed that 27% of the population believed in reincarnation, and that believers came quite evenly from main stream Christian denominations. In 2009 Dr Jim B.

Tucker, who worked with Stevenson published a 250 page account of his work.

Walter Semkiv was a medical doctor who discovered as a student that he had psychic abilities. Being a sceptic he took little interest. One evening in 1984, however, when he had nothing to do, he was persuaded to attend a medium sitting. In the course of the sitting a spirit guide, speaking through the medium who was in a full trance, told him that, in a previous life he was the famous John Adams, first Vice President of the US under Washington, then the second President of the US. He dismissed the information as ridiculous.

He chose to make a career as a consultant to industry and eventually became a medical director of Unocal 76, an oil company. In 1995 he was fully engaged in his medical career. One day out of the blue, while waiting for colleagues in Honolulu, a booming voice inside his head commanded: "Study the lifetime of Adams". Dr. Semkiv found the voice "firm and undeniable, and powerful enough to make me go to a bookstore in Honolulu". That decision changed his life.

He became a researcher of reincarnations, set up a website (_www.iisis.net_), publicised Ian Stevenson's research findings and established a worldwide network to search for authentic reincarnation cases.

IISIS is the Institute for the Integration of Science, Intuition and Spirit. On its website it publishes information on all cases where its governing committee decides that their strict criteria have been met. These criteria became the international standard for the authenticity of such cases.

Dr. Semkiv has also written a number of books on reincarnation which have been published internationally. In addition he has been a presenter at the first four World Congresses for Regression Therapy, held in the Netherlands, India, Brazil and Turkey. He has been featured on CNN and in *Newsweek*.

Interest in the work of IISIS quickly spread. Other similar websites who apply the same criteria have been set up. IISIS monitors and grades these websites. All this information is accessible on IISIS's website. There is no overall figure for properly validated cases but in 2015 they would have to be numbered in hundreds, if not more.

Near-Death Experiences.

Near-Death experiences have a history as old as folklore. The first significant written account was Raymond Moody's 1975 paperback, in which Moody set out the criteria for authentic near-death experiences. Beyond that important step the book itself was not considered to be a scientific investigation.

Dr. Pym van Pommel is a world-renowned cardiologist. Since his initial study of near-death experience, which was published in the prestigious medical journal *The Lancet* he has been researching reincarnation. His 2010 paperback of 414 pages established itself as the leading scientific investigation into near-death experiences.

A number of people who were interested in this area had each modified Moody's criteria. Van Pommel examined them and developed a set of criteria which were very close to that of Moody's. In the meantime he had organised a network, consisting of hospitals and other institutions, where the medical staff of doctors and nurses were happy to record details of near-death experiences which they personally witnessed. Now he could send them report forms on which they could rate each experience witnessed against all his selected criteria.

With these reports he was in a position to amend his criteria but they remained close to those of Moody. His book presents a full analysis of all reports received by him. It was acclaimed by the Washington Post and by very many leading researchers in this field. He has resigned his post as a practicing cardiologist to devote his time to further research and lecturing all over the world. He may be visited online at www.pimvanlommet.nl.

Jeffrey Long, M. D., has served on the board of directors of the international association for Near-Death studies and established the non-profit Near-Death Experience Research Foundation and the NDERF website. His 2011 paperback with Paul Perry, *Evidence of the Afterlife,* has 215 pages. It was a *New York Times* best seller.

The most recent of his NDERF surveys, is presented in this book. 613 cases from around the world are analysed. All had rating scores of 7 or more out of 10. He selected twelve elements as follows:

1.   Out-of-body experience (OBE): Separation of consciousness from the physical body.
2.   Heightened senses
3.   Intense and generally positive emotions or feelings
4.   Passing into or through a tunnel
5.   Encountering a mystical or brilliant light
6.   Encountering other beings, either mystical beings or deceased relatives or friends
7.   A sense of alteration of time or space
8.   Life review
9.   Encountering unworldly ("heavenly") realms
10.   Encountering or learning special knowledge
11.   Encountering a boundary or barrier
12.   A return to the body, either voluntary or involuntary

Long also reported that near-death experiences are remarkably consistent around the world; that after-effects are often powerful and lasting; and that the stages follow a consistent pattern.

In a minority of cases, near-death experiences and their after-effects are disturbing and can require psychiatric attention.

What We Have Learned About the Afterworld.

1.   In general we have learned that inhabitants of the Afterworld are like ourselves, except that they normally do not have our physical bodies.

2.   Those who have communicated have a level of awareness which is incomparably greater then ours. That applies to the more normal contacts made by loving mothers, such as "Little Friedel do you hear me."

3.   The Scole experiment has demonstrated that some of them have reached an extraordinary level of awareness and are seasoned participants in the World of Cosmic Consciousness.

4.   Because of cultural conditioning we earthlings find it almost impossible to accept established facts about the state of their existence.

5.   We need to strengthen our language about them in a way that expresses the similarities of their minds to our own.

6.   There is evidence that some of the After-lifers have the ability to generate a body which looks exactly like a human body, talks like us, walks like us, and eats like us, and if we shake their hands, they feel like us. But their bodies are made, not of the same animal substances as ours but of a plasma which is fully mouldable.

7.   Reincarnates are us. They do everything like us, including marrying and having children. While they often have physical resemblances to the person they were in a previous life, validated cases show that they may born to a family who lives in a different culture, and has a different religion. They may also be of a

different sex. Mostly they live pretty normal lives but often develop a talent which was notable in their previous life.

8. Validated cases show that some re-incarnates achieve spiritual greatness in their earthly lives. In these cases the mother may receive a clear message in a dream, and their birth may be heralded by special events. I believe an angel delivered such a message to Mary. The wise men from the East, where reincarnation was more widely accepted, may have been highly spiritual men, or angels, or may even have been re-incarnates themselves.

For references visit www.isiis.ie

What We Don't Know About the Afterworld

1. Apart from the Scole experiment, messages from the Afterworld have told us nothing about its internal communications except that we do not have the ability to understand them. It must be assumed that what is not known is vastly greater than what is known. Hence we can only speculate metaphorically about its internal activities.

2. So far only its creative aspects have been discussed. It has, however a sinister province. That province has manifested itself most clearly through the Ouija Board. There are many examples of people with an addictive trait whose lives have been destroyed by addiction to the Ouija Board. The usual interpretation is that they have been targeted by evil spirits. For this reason the Christian Churches have condemned this practice as dangerous.

3. The question arises: Who are these evil spirits. Are they persons who were born on earth; are they the fallen angels; do they inhabit our Supernormal world; or do they live in a world of their own with powers to inhabit our normal world; what is their relationship to God? We don't have answers.

4. Will science provide more information? These evil beings do not like the truth. Far from co-operating authentically, they will

quasi-cooperate with a view to creating as much confusion as possible.

5. If they are of the same substance as guardian angels they will exist in a realm which lies outside Nature and hence outside the laws of any kind of science.

Summary
Looking back over the last half century at Trans-communication, Reincarnation, and Near-Death Experiences, I cannot but recall words from the last message of the Scole Experiments:
"The links that were made have already enabled inter-dimensional energies and wisdom to assist the changes to future earth consciousness."

Are the new vistas in science already coming to pass; is earth consciousness already changing inevitably, despite the many enemies that are determined to halt that progress.

Notable is the fact that, while the reincarnations which were validated were mainly cases of religiosts, there were also cases of naturalists. Ref. (*www.iisis.net*)

Notable also is the fact that there are a number of global secular movements which have achieved practical successes in recent decades, and whose aim is human development. For both religiosts and naturalists that aim converges with spiritual development. The most advanced of these movements are: the human capabilities movement, the EC mental health improvement movement, the flourishing movement. These and other movements will be discussed in Chapter 10.

Chapter 6
Cosmic Consciousness

Introduction

In the Western World, contemporary vistas in Cosmic Consciousness have been pioneered by Dr Ervin Laszlo, over the last four decades. I first came across Dr. Laszlo's work forty years ago when I was researching systems engineering concepts. At that time he was already recognized internationally for his research publications in both engineering and in systems theory.

In his "latest and perhaps most definitive book", *The Self Actualizing Uuniverse,* 2014, he presents the latest scientifically theorized and experimentally investigated work by him and his colleagues. There are a number of publications in the field of CC. Because Laszlo's work is so highly developed, and because it is so well presented in his 2014, 200-page paperback, I have chosen it for discussion and consider it to be essential reading for anyone who has not already read it. A brief summary follows.

The Akasha and the Akashic Field

"The tenet that the observed world is a manifestation of a deeper dimension is now rediscovered at the cutting edge of quantum field physics. It is not new: it has been a basic element in classical Indian philosophy. Samkhya, one of the earliest philosophical teachings in India, held that there is a compendium of knowledge and information conserved in a nonphysical plane of reality, referred to as the Akashic Records. The Akasha is the fundamental element. It holds the other elements in itself, but it is also outside of them, for it is beyond space and time. According to Paramahansa Yogananda, the Akasha is the subtle background against which everything in the material universe becomes perceptible." Ref. B13.

Belief in such a cosmology was also widespread in the same era in what is now known as Argentina. It has been frequently proposed in the Western World in the last two millennia. A number of contemporary philosophers and scientists, baffled at the emergence of consciousness from unconscious matter, have suggested that some form of natural consciousness preceded matter. One of these is Professor Keith Ward, a Christian philosopher.

Dr. Keith Ward

"I propose that consciousness, though in the human case it is a factor that emerges from the physical development of the brain, is an irreducible fact, like energy or matter. A conscious state is not just a physical state. It has its own proper reality, and no account of reality that ignores it can be complete.

Though animal and human conscious states emerge from complex brains, they are truly emergent, new sorts of reality, and they stand in need of an explanation that cannot be reduced to physical terms alone. **It is hard to imagine that there could be conscious states within the universe before brains evolve, so such states would have to exist outside our space-time, or as some sort of potential-for-consciousness, to be realized when physical conditions have become complex enough. Put another way, mind is prior to matter. Mind causes matter to exist".** Ref. A11.

Here Keith Ward is writing about the Akasha, something that was created by God, existed before our Big Bang, and is a natural entity. He does not mention anything natural that corresponds to the Akashic Field.

The Akashic Field

Laszlo, in describing his scientific theorizing and his work of experimental validation, writes purely as a scientist. He does not mention anything supernatural. He first refers to the phenomenon of quantum entanglement. He then goes to describe the latest findings about it.

"This kind of entanglement is not limited to the quantum domain: it surfaces also at macroscopic scales. Life would not be possible in its absence. In the human body, for example, trillions of cells need to be fully and precisely correlated to maintain the organism in its physically highly improbable living state. **This calls for quasi-instant multidimensional connection throughout the organism.**

Yet another finding that cannot be explained by the currant paradigm is that organic molecules are produced in stars. It appears that the laws that govern existence and evolution in the universe are fine-tuned to produce the kind of complex systems we associate with the phenomena of life."

Laszlo goes on to consider the properties of the nonlocal interaction generating field. "Following the hypothetico-deductive method of theory construction in science, these properties can be first "invented", but then they must be tested against observations. They can be considered verified when they provide the simplest consistent explanation of the observations. We apply this principle to the field presumed to generate nonlocal interactions in nature. The following properties are ascribed to the field":

Universality (the field is present and active at all points in space and time)

Nonvectorial effectiveness (the field produces effect through nonvectorial in-formation)

Holographic information storage (information in the field is carried in a distributed form, with the totality of the information present at all points)

Supraluminal effect-propagation (the field produces effects quasi-instantly at all finite distances)

Laszlo continues: "Fields are not observables: only their effects can be observed and measured. They share this quality with all the laws and regularities of nature. We observe a dynamically evolving, actualizing universe, but we do not observe the laws and regularities that "drive" it. Cause and effect cannot be collapsed because the effect is manifest while the cause is not – or it is only indirectly so."

"Scores of philosophers have maintained that the observed world is rooted in a real but unobservable dimension. Philosophers of the mystical branch in Greek metaphysics—the Idealists and the Eleatic school (including thinkers such as Pythagoras, Plato, Parmenides, and Plotinus)—differed on many points but were united in the affirmation of a "hidden" dimension.

The dimension that generates the holographic spacetime we experience is the Akasha. The Akasha harbors the geometrical relations that govern the interaction of quanta and of all things constituted of quanta in space and time. It is the seat of the fields and forces of the manifest world. The Akasha is the universal gravitational field that attracts things proportionately to their mass; it is the electromagnetic field that conveys electric and magnetic effects through space; it is the ensemble of the quantum fields that assigns probabilities to the behavior of quanta; and it is the scalar holofield that creates nonlocal interaction among quanta and configurations of quanta. The Akasha is the integration of all these elements in a unitary cosmic dimension that is beyond space and time. It is the fundamental, if in the everyday context hidden, dimension of the world." (Laszlo)

Trans-communication Between the Six Worlds of Awareness Which Constitute Nature.

How does the world of CC interact with the other five worlds? Laszlo does not deal with this difficult question; yet the answer seems to be fundamental before the existence of this sixth world can be asserted. In other words what work does it do that cannot be ascribed to the Afterworld which already has persons with the highest level of awareness, God excluded?

In this section we can only speak metaphorically. Most of the words we use are inapplicable to communication within the Supernormal world.

In Chapter 5, we reasoned that the delegation could be persons who lived at the highest level of divinity in the Afterworld, and who could be assigned temporarily to the world of CC. But could they not do the same work from their home base in the Afterworld, if they were just temporarily assigned to projects. Is the world of CC not simply redundant? Laszlo, who is described on the back cover of his 2014 book, "as the most important cosmologist alive today" gives his answer below.

Laszlo's Cosmology

In Part 1 of his 2014 book, Laszlo presents a detailed critique of classic cosmologies. In Part 1V he posits an Akasha cosmology.

The Big Bang happened "Through the action of the repulsive forces that arose when the collapsing prior universe reached quantum dimensions". . . . . It was "a phase transition between universes, or phases of the multi-verse; not a Big Bang, but a Big Bounce."

"Before the Big Bang there was a preceding universe or phase of the multi-verse, with physical properties similar to that of our own.

The process we see as basic to life originated as coherent

relations emerged in time in the rich welter of organic molecules on the watery surface of some satellites in orbit around active stars," writes Laszlo.

"Consciousness did not "arise" – it has always been present as an aspect of the intrinsically psychophysical universe.

What is the nature of consciousness? It is the mental, more exactly "mindlike", aspect of the matterlike systems in the manifest dimension of the universe; a display or reflection of the information contained in the universe's A-dimension."

"The physical constants have the values they now have because they have been progressively evolved in the preceding cycles of the multiverse and were passed on to our universe in the phase transition we recognize as a Big Bounce.

The universe's forces are not limited to four: the force (or field) responsible for nonlocal interation is as basic and universal as the four classical fields, and there are various quantum fields and forces as well". (Laszlo)

"After the body dies life appears to persist as a form of consciousness in the Akasha, and can be experienced and communicated with, as shown in near-death exeriences, after-death communications, and medium-transmitted contact.

Which book provides the best answer, Classic science or Akasha science. **There is no single book nor is there ever likely to be one, although some books offer better answers than others today, and very likely in the future".**

Ervin Laszlo's Philosophy

Laszlo ends Part 1 of his 2014 book with the following statement on his philosophy.

"Ever more people, especially young people, are rediscovering their oneness with each other and with the world. They are rediscovering the power of love—rediscovering that love is more than the desire for sexual union, that it is a profound sense of belonging to each other and to the cosmos. This rediscovery is timely, and it is not mere fantasy: it has its roots in our holographically whole, nonlocally interconnected universe. Love is the way to supercoherence. Achieving it is health enhancing and socially and ecologically sound. It gives rise to behaviors and aspirations that are good for us, good for others, and good for the world. Supercoherence is objectively good. It is the highest value philosophers called "The Good.""

His engagement by Princeton University to advise their Department of Humanities on establishing an undergraduate course on the philosophical aspects of Cosmic Consciousness is a measure of the importance attached by that university to his philosophy. Leading universities around the world are following its example.

PART 111
The Supernatural Realm

INTERMISSION 2

DOES A WORLD AWASH WITH PAIN DENY A LOVING CREATOR?

This emotionally loaded question has been the elephant in the religiost room for over a century. However it is a diverson from the central aims of this book which opens by saying that proof of a supernatural supreme being whose abode is a spiritual realm is logically impossible.

This small book has more realistic aims. These are firstly to acquaint the reader with the new vistas in religions and spiritualities which have been opened up by philosophers, theologians, and new sciences over the last five decades or so. Secondly it hoped to show that the volume of CQ evidence and SV evidence for the existence of an Afterlife is so massive that it puts beyond all reasonable doubt that an Afterlife exists.

1. Naturalists have not produced reasoned argument that there is no afterlife. Their own position is precisely one of faith-belief: who can possibly *know* that there are no souls who go to some kind of Supernormal Afterlife beyond our ken, to live on eternally as spiritual persons. As we saw in the first page of this book, evidential proof that a coherent (no internal contradictions) reality does not exist is a logical impossibility and the Afterlife is certainly a coherent possibility.

Naturalists do, however, have evidence of substance that a loving Creator God cannot be both omnipotent and loving. Here they can point to an internal contradiction: a world awash with gratuitous pain created by an omnipotent and loving Creator.

Something has to give. Religiosts have put great effort and logical reasoning into their belief that suffering has eternal benefits, by way of soul-making, which completely outweigh sufferings that are relatively of infinitesimal duration; furthermore an infinitely just God will see that every soul gets equal justice.

Many religiosts just don't buy this argument and dismiss it as sophistry. They say that here we have a mystery which we must accept, as Russell and Feyman said of the impossibility of our cosmos self-generating out of absolute nothingness.

2. Alternatively we must question the omnipotence of the Abrahamic God. One of the most fruitful new vistas in religion does this: it proposes a loving God who has relinquished a small -- but for us vital – part of his omnipotence *because He wishes his new species of being to have the maximum freedom of choice*

Each human would then be free to work with God's plan or to reject his plan, as the fallen angels did. The only two creations of beings in which we religiosts believe – the Angels and the human species -- were made by a God who relinquished part of his omnipotence in the act of creating free beings.

If God held back the gift of free-will, he would be limiting the creativity of his created beings. Would an altruistic loving mother or father limit their children's creativity? We are God's children – to limit our creativity, or our capacity for altruistic love, would be to deprive us of his two great gifts to our species.

Does God share our pains? Knowing that he was creating a random world that would almost certainly be awash with pain he would, like every mother and father, know that he would necessarily share our pains, and our joys.

Did he have to create a random world where everything that could happen, would happen? I accept the traditional argument here, that a world where there was regulation, such as 'pain for children under x years of age ruled out', would make it obvious that there was a puppet master behind the screen limiting our choice, and diminishing our freedom and creativity.

Do we need suffering if we are to grow spiritually? The old school wisdom-slogan says, 'No gain without pain'. Indeed it is hard to imagine that spiritual growth could take place if human life was a bed of roses where everything was given on request. Once more the innate urge of an altruistic mother or father is to encourage a robust sense of responsibility and altruism by developing 'habits of the heart' in their children whereby they can cope creatively with the nasty things in our world - loving altruism-forming habits such as 'caring and sharing'

A world awash with pain has been a leading issue for the past year or so on RTE TV discussion panels and on one to one interviews. A number of books have also been published giving the authors personal experience. These personal accounts add great poignancy to the issue. The emotional temperature can rise to extreme heights at one end of the scale -- particularly where children are concerned – to a coping acceptance at the low end.

I give below three TV interviews and comments, followed by more general accounts and overall comments.

The first TV interview was on Gay Byrne's RTE 1 series – *The Meaning of Life.* The interviewee was Stephen Fry, a world famous theatrical figure and popular TV presenter. Stephen is a big man with a commanding presence and an even more commanding and entertaining flow of words. When Gay asked his standard final question, "What would you say to God if he was there at the Pearly Gate" [leading into Heaven], Stephen launched into a blistering attack on God. Fuming with extreme outrage he delivered his assault with magnificent oratory. He threw everything at God, his knock out blow being those bacteria which sometimes enter the eyes of children and eat out their eyes over a long period, leaving them blind for life.

Gay looked on bemused. Later he said that after many years presenting the *Meaning of Life*, Stephen's answer was by far the longest one he received.

The significance of this particular episode was its international impact on Face book. An enormous number of participants were engaged for days discussing it. A great majority applauded Fry. Women being emotionally richer than men they well outnumbered the men. The newspapers reported that amongst the women there was a big majority of young girls.

My immediate personal reaction was one of annoyance (there go the emotions) that Fry was telling the world's religiosts, a majority of the world population; that Western religiosts worshipped a pathological tyrant.

Shortly after Stephen Fry's episode, singer Mary Black was Gay's interviewee. Recently turned sixty she still easily holds her place in the top echelon of popular Irish singers. She also has a big international reputation. Her beauty is untypical, and her magnificent voice and stage presence exude a sincerity, and a flavour of mysticism of which she has always been aware, as she revealed in the interview.

She knows she has had a charmed life: a loving, musical family who recognised her unique talent as a child and gave her every possible support from their scanty resource. As a teenage singer she was noted by talent scouts and was on her way to fame in her early teens. International touring soon followed with great success. She has had, and still has, the same happy marriage, with two lovely and successful daughters whom she adores. What more could anyone wish for?

When asked the usual last question: what will you say to God when you die and find him there at the Pearly Gate – the same question which provoked Stephen Fry's outrage – her answer was short and simple: "what about the children?"

Now it was my turn to be bemused. After giving God credit throughout the preceding interview for her very fortunate life, why would she now give God such a short answer? One can speculate about different reasons – that I leave as an interesting exercise for each reader – but she alone can know the full truth, and that only by an in-depth probe of her mind.

True, she started the interview by saying she was going through a confused state of spirituality. I wager that, "on mature reflection" she will regret her short sentence to God. There was no comment from Gay but, in contrast to Stephen Fry's answer, he must have found it one of the shortest answers ever given to his final question

My third interviewee was Mickey Harte, the manager of the winning Co. Tyrone Gaelic Football team, on Pat Kenny's first UTV Ireland series in May 1915. His only daughter, his beloved daughter Michaela, was murdered by an intruder in her five star hotel in Mauritius on the second day of her honeymoon. Pat Kenny questioned him deeply but kindly on how he survived the immediate trauma and the long drawn out suffering of the investigation and trial.

His answer was given with great grief and striking sincerity. God and Michaela brought him through. He had felt her close presence since she died, telling him what she wanted: that he continue his life with the Tyrone football team in the same way that he and she had always done.

He realised that he had received a wonderful gift from God in the joyful years with Michaela and their joint involvement with the Tyrone team. His life had also been blessed by God in many other ways. All in all, he could not complain. Tragedy had strengthened him in his love for God, and brought a sense of serenity he had not previously known. This from a man who had lost a very talented daughter just as she was about to launch on a wonderful new phase of her life.

With parents who lost a child -- especially if the child was disabled -- the happiness of knowing, loving, and caring for a child throughout her or his life, however short or long, was the predominant theme.

This obtained for non-believing parents also. Normal, healthy naturalists love life particularly if they embrace a well-developed humanist philosophy.

Joan and I experienced the completely unexpected loss of a son at the age of twenty four. He was due to sit his M.A in Philosophy a few weeks later. He was healthy, vibrant and full of creative energy and fun. A cramp while swimming in a cold inland lake on a magnificent June day, cost him his life.

He and Joan were particularly close. She was devastated for a year before stability returned. She achieved this in a few sessions with an excellent counselling therapist --   without any medication or addictive substances of any kind. She knew she had to do this for the sake of the family.

I too was initially traumatised but realised that I must keep going as normally as possible for everyone's sake. My religious faith was not strong at the time. I accepted that we lived in a random world and that this is what just happened. Continuing activity was my life-line.

As a religiost I did believe in an afterlife and felt that Peter was not far away. I prayed to him for help and apologised for the many times I failed to behave with him as a loving father should behave. Had my faith been stronger and if I had believed in reincarnation as I now do, it would have been much easier to accept such a loss.

Returning to the Stephen Fry episode, it stands apart from the other accounts I have heard. Considered objectively, the example he gave of innocent suffering merits some comments.

1. At the time Jesus lived leprosy was common and so were leprous children who died young from their disease. In pagan cultures infanticide was widely practised in the case of disabled or unhealthy newborns. Nomads who live in a harsh environment left their children to die.

2. Today millions of children suffer pain and die very young of malnutrition and disease in many countries. A huge amount of pain occurs because of the failure of our affluent Western cultures to take the necessary steps to help these poorer cultures. Imagine the money that would be available to reduce suffering if the huge amounts of money spent on wars and space projects were diverted to medical research and to various aids. We know what God wants us to do. Is it not we who fail both God and the world's poorest.

Modern religiosts who believe that all who live decently receive a warm welcome to the Afterlife would expect that all young children who die would go directly, without any further pain, to a joyful and happy development home in the Afterlife; when they mature they would have an option of reincarnation.

Perhaps Steven Fry should join Bob Geldorf on Bob's campaign of fund-raising for the poor of Africa and other poverty-stricken areas. Maybe he has already done so. He certainly would be an asset to any such campaign.

Afterwards my emotional reaction to Stephen Fry's TV performance disturbed me. His outrage was extreme but that was his style. Why should I be annoyed. Then I recalled that I had always thought of Stephen as a big-hearted generous man. If that was so, then whatever he thought of God, God would love him.

I began to feel that, on leaving the tunnel of light and entering the presence of Jesus the volatile and highly intelligent Stephen would immediately realise how mistaken he had been. He would have a good laugh at himself. Jesus would surely join him in that laugh as they planned the way forward for him. Perhaps God himself would join in the laughter, as the great mystic theologian Meister Eckhart imagined centuries ago.

Chapter 7
Histories of God.

Introduction

This is the first of two chapters which deals with the various concepts of God which have emerged from the Axial Age, during which a great transformation occurred in human spiritual awareness. It can be seen as the first Enlightenment. It is written for those who feel that their knowledge of the spiritual history of this period is inadequate. It is not required reading for those who are familiar with the period.

The Axial Age.

I am taking the Axial Age as the two millennia BCE in which a number of great religions and philosophies emerged in different countries from the Western Mediterranean region to the Far East. Differing in many of their concepts of the Supernatural, they all shared similar core concepts. These core concepts have underpinned those Axial Age religions which have endured for over two millennia and become universal religions for the many as well as for the few.

As well as an enriched concept of compassion, the Axial Age religions also shared a belief in a transcendent moral order, be it the Chinese Way of Heaven, the Hindu Brahman, the Egyptian Divine King, the Buddhist Dharmakaya, or the Abrahamic Heaven where one almighty God ruled. This concept also surfaced in Greek philosophy as Plato's form of the Good, Aristotle's deism and teleology, Stoic concepts of Fate, and Philo of Alexandria's

Logos. A transcendent moral order was conceived as *the* order that *all humans, rulers and subjects alike*, should seek to understand and emulate.

The Good Life and The Afterworld

The concepts of compassion, and of a transcendent moral order, led to two beliefs that enormously increased the appeal of the Axial religions. The first was the belief that a life lived in harmony with a Divine order would be the most fulfilled earthly life. The second belief, given the almost universal belief in some kind of afterlife, was that a benign moral order would, in justice, reward those who had lived virtuously in their previous lives. While neither strand of thought reflects pure altruism, both have helped to move human behaviour from egotism toward altruism.

Thus authentic religious movements have always had two clear and fundamental distinguishing characteristics; they have put personal transcendence from egotism at the top of their agendas; they have also promoted the concept of a transcendent moral order and catered for the needs of those who feel an affinity with, and draw special inspiration from, such a concept.

Christianity, Judaism, and Buddhism are the most prominent Axial religions in contemporary Western culture. All three have emphatically endorsed religious tolerance vis-à-vis other religions. There is also a clear trend towards tolerance within their own folds; Western Buddhism does not insist that an adherent believe in reincarnation, and Christianity tacitly accepts that it has adherents who are inspired by the teachings of Jesus but have problems with the concept of an only Son of God, and even, perhaps with the idea of a transcendent realm.

All three, however, can justify their claim that belief in a transcendent realm offers a special source of moral inspiration – not as a substitute for any of the authentic sources of inspiration that are open to naturalists, but by adding an extra dimension of meaning to those sources.

And they can provide rational and irrefutable arguments that the weight of reason, as well as intuition, tips the scales towards belief in a transcendent realm. They accept that their arguments are not compelling and that atheists can provide contra-arguments that are also rational and irrefutable.

Naturalists dismiss the idea of a transcendent moral order. Physicist Steven Weinberg claims: "It's not a moral order out there, it's something we impose." But, according to evolutionary psychologist Robert Wright, the history of the last five millennia shows clearly that we have failed dismally, time and time again, to impose a moral order.

Going back millions of years to a pre-religion era, he says that the caring morality which enabled small groups of our hunter-gatherer ancestors to survive was *imposed on them* by the exigencies of life's evolutionary process; and, today, we as a species are again being told, perhaps for the last time: accept *the* moral order or become extinct.

Wright has himself evolved over the past sixteen years from firm agnosticism to agnosticism-with-a-leaning: "The fact that there's a moral order out there doesn't mean there's a God. On the other hand, it's evidence in favour of the God hypothesis and evidence against Weinberg's worldview. . . . What's more, though believing in this moral order doesn't make you a believer in God, it may make you in some sense, religious. . . when we were looking for a definition of religion broad enough to encompass the many things that have been called religion, we settled on a formulation by William James. Religious belief, he said, "consists of the belief that there is an unseen order, and that our supreme good lies in harmoniously adjusting ourselves thereto.""

This is also the basic belief of mainstream Stoicism

Transformative Movements and Human Corruptibility

In his 2009 book, *Born to Be Good,* Dacher Keltner draws on the latest neuroscience, as well as on evolutionary psychology and contemporary social studies, to present compelling evidence that compassion is extensively hardwired into the nervous system of the normal human being. In ordinary everyday life people continuously act in ways that are compassionate and altruistic; there are solid historical grounds for assuming that they always did – even in adverse conditions. Compassionate activities are intrinsically rewarding, as the Axial sages knew. Why then has the Axial Agenda run into the sand?

The answer seems to be that egotism and self-deception are also parts of our evolutionary heritage that are extensively grounded in our psyches; they have proved intransigently resistant to transcendence. Attempts to create social environments favourable to morality have had little success. Wars and oppression have continued to provide breeding grounds that are conducive to egotism and violence.

Secondly religious movements have had grievous failures of leadership. Most notably, the leaders of Christianity have tried to impose its dogmas – at times even using direct and indirect violence in pursuit of their goals – in flagrant contradiction to the teachings of its founder and the practices of its early-centuries communities. They have also engaged in ill-advised conflicts with science. The results have been catastrophic for the Axial Agenda which was based on free individual commitment.

Religious movements are not the only transformative movements which have been betrayed by their leaders. Twentieth century secular transformative movements have produced a combined death-toll which historians reckon could be of the order of ninety million lives, with related suffering inflicted on multiples of that number – all in little more than half a century.

We cannot, however, outlaw all transformative movements because so many of them have been betrayed by their all-too-human leaders. On the contrary, history is now telling us, more than ever, that we need secular movements which promote socialist insights of egalitarianism, solidarity, and human development; it also tells us that past abuses that arose under perverted socialist ideologies must never re-occur. Likewise, we need religious movements which will cultivate the needs of the many who have authentic religious sensibilities; but we must insist that they too reject all policies of imposition.

Tolerant religious movements which are driven by the Axial insights and "put the abandonment of selfishness and the spirituality of compassion at the top of their agenda", continue to have a creative role in achieving the good society. There are many indications that this view will continue.

Throughout history the social value of religious movements has been recognized by wise regimes. Progressive Chinese Emperors gathered sages from all religions around their courts. Pagan regimes saw religions as a source of social cohesion and support for morality, and, while they slaughtered and enslaved their enemies, they adopted their gods into their own pantheon. Today, both the Chinese and Russian regimes have abandoned atheism as a desirable political goal; they are encouraging tolerant religious movements while ensuring the preservation of a secular state. The USA, the most secular state in the Western World, is also the most religious; as the Founding Fathers foresaw, religious movements can best flourish within a tolerant secular state.

Religious individuals and movements have an obligation of conscience to oppose publicly those social policies which they believe are hostile to the Axial Agenda; indeed, they should be encouraged to do so, even by those who do not share their religious beliefs.

Where differences arise between religious and secular movements, both sides should welcome dialogue with respect for each other's insights. When necessary the state must legislate, respecting all human rights as best it can. In a pluralist democratic society, intolerance, be it religious or atheistic, must be rejected.

Western Liberal Democracies and the Axial Agenda

Within contemporary Western liberal democracies, peace reigns if we exclude spasmodic terrorism, the Axial religions promote tolerance, and totalitarian socialism has been put to rest. Traditional slavery (but not all forms of slavery) has been abolished. Individuals have unprecedented freedom of behaviour in their personal lives – a freedom guaranteed by social acceptance and legal protection of human rights.

It would seem that we have the ideal environment in which to progress the Axial Agenda. Yet we have Gorbachev's disturbing warning that 'a deep, profoundly intelligent and inherently humane European culture is retreating to the background before the primitive revelry of violence and pornography.' (quoted in *The Politics of Hope* by Jonathan Sacks, 2000).

It is easy to add a litany of social ills which would support Gorbachev's basic contention: alcohol and drug abuse, family breakdown, violence, child abuse, psychiatric illness, growing prison populations, mindless celebrity adulation, obesity, etc., etc.

Gorbachev was speaking of a Europe in which, for over half a century, secular political regimes which espoused egalitarianism, solidarity and human development, have been in control. Educational systems have been secularised, made universally available and developed to extraordinary heights. The influence of the churches in the public sphere has been dramatically reduced.

It is clear that affluent, peaceful, and liberal societies are also fertile breeding grounds for egotism and greed. In fact, they offer unending opportunities and huge financial incentives to increasing numbers of those who are ready to exploit the less desirable features of our evolutionary heritage. Our media keep us very well aware of the illegal exploitations that are pervasive in our societies.

We are much less aware of, and much more accepting of, the widespread legal exploitation of our egotism and greed, something that has long been a part of our economic culture and has now become its driving force. We have, unwittingly, allowed ourselves to be persuaded that "greed is good", that to deny this maxim is to deny the good life.

Yet as Keltner points out, and as we all know from experience, people in their everyday lives commonly perform spontaneous acts of altruism. Donations to charities are a universal feature of contemporary cultures. Every survey shows that people find compassionate activities rewarding. The Axial challenge remains: how to induce more and more individuals to put the abandonment of selfishness and the spirituality of compassion at the top of their agenda, thus counteracting the morally destructive forces that can operate freely in a liberal society.

Secular states have a major role to play in supporting this transformative agenda by providing resources for an appropriate educational system and by creating a more congenial social environment. Given the large numbers who feel no affinity with a transcendent realm, secular movements with a similar transformative agenda also have a major role to play. Wise regimes and wise civic movements would encourage all authentic transformative movements, both religious and secular. We need all the creative resources that can be mustered.

The time has come for an open-minded evaluation of the Great Enlightenment. Certainly it has made a massive contribution to freedom of expression, but its enthronement of reason as the master over intuition and emotion has impoverished the Western mind.

Chapter 8
The Evolution of Christianity

Introduction
This is the second of two introductory chapters to Chapter 9.

Its purpose is to provide some basic historical data on the most relevant changes in the evolution of Christian beliefs in the millennia since the coming of Jesus. It is optional reading for those who already feel reasonably well informed in this area.

GENISIS
In ancient times there were a myriad of creation stories.

Genesis is the most durable and influential. It begins with Abraham c.1700 BCE. It was a scholarly oral tradition until c.700 BCE when it was first written into the Bible c.700 BCE. Seen by the scholars as an inspiring story based on facts, they sought to bring greater coherence into their written version through the usual method of open dialogue amongst themselves.

Knowing that, for the educated, faith and reason must comply, they soon began a continual reinterpretation in the light of changing events. This was particularly so after the destruction of the temple and the full colonisation of Israel.

Greeks and Manicheans
While the Rabbis were applying reason to revelation the first rational speculations of Classical Greece were being applied to existing nature in the 6th century BCE. Starting from primordial matter their theories were evolutionary. They reached the first

stages of a scientific cosmology. Science and particularly mathematics were given primacy. The Greeks also excelled in applying reason to logic, ethics and politics (e.g. Socrates, Plato, and Aristotle). They had their own concept of revelation which has withstood the test of time. However, they did not develop a cohesive theory of creation.

The Roman Stoics, who had many notable followers, endured well into the Christian era. They had a revival during the Enlightenment period, and now have contemporary followers.

In her book, *The Therapy of Desire*, 1998, Professor Martha Nussbaum, an eminent scholar in ancient Greek and Roman cultures, shows how the Stoics followed the Greek tradition of applying holistic medical terms to 'sicknesses of the soul' – their term for harmful unruly desires. Greek doctors found in their practices, that ailments that seemed to be physical were in fact psychosomatic and needed therapy of the soul for a lasting cure.

Such a cure required the lifelong practice of self-therapy from the patient. The highly educated Stoics dialogued together and developed an expert therapy as shown in their meetings, letters and memoirs. It had a high spiritual content which was based on a form of Panentheism. In the opinion of Nussbaum, who is herself an eminent practical psychologist, their therapy compares more than favourably with modern therapies.

With the decline of classical paganism, the well-established faith of the Manicheans offered the most serious challenge to the Jewish/Christian story of creation. That faith taught a complex dualistic cosmology describing the struggle between a good spiritual world of light and an evil material world of darkness. Over a few centuries Christianity succeeded in reducing it to a secretive esoteric faith in the West. In the Eastern World it continued to have a robust public existence for many centuries, but today has few adherents.

Christian Biblical Re-Interpretations, Old and New

Christian scholars continued the Judaic tradition of reinterpretation for further centuries until the Papacy achieved and rigorously applied full control of official Christian beliefs with the recognition of Pope Leo (The Great) as the final authority over all Christian bishops, both East and West. Henceforth scholars had to have his consent.

Since Vatican II in the 1960s the rigidity of Papal control has been gradually relaxed by Pope John XXIII and his successors. In the past few decades the possibility of a much more open dialogue between the Papacy and the theologians has been opened up by a minority of Christian scholars.

These are declaring both their full commitment to their Christian Faiths, to the mission of their own Christian Churches, and to national and international dialogue with other Religions. The days of excommunication for public declarations of beliefs that are unorthodox has happily gone. Sanctions on theologians, however, still occur but are frequently denounced by what seems to be a majority of Christians of every kind: a delicate situation.

Contemporary Interpretations of Genesis

In its modern form the core beliefs of Genesis are:

1. The one eternal and perfect God conceived, created, and guides us and our universe.

2. *Out of nothing* He created it at a time of his choice.

3 He created man and woman in his own image and likeness to care for His creation, and to progress its evolution.

The number of respected denominations around the world who worship the Abrahamic God runs into the hundreds (most of them in the US). They all differ in their interpretations, but on the above core beliefs of Genesis they have a consensus. On the Mosaic commandments there is a similar consensus.

A Very Brief History of Judaism Since 600 BCE

In the six centuries before Christ the Jews, as a people, suffered a series of subjugations by surrounding empires. Eventually the Roman Empire finally destroyed the temple and dispersed the Jews. Thus began the Jewish diaspora. This tragedy made them more determined than ever to preserve the sacred Jewish culture of a chosen people.

Now without their cherished synagogues, they practiced prescribed religious rituals daily in their homes. Other prescribed memorial days of special prayers and meals were held on certain days. These practices continue to this day and assure their survival as a people, while so many once powerful Empires and peoples no longer exist.

The Jews did not begin to develop a coherent theory of the Afterworld until the third century BCE.

In his acclaimed book, *The Great Partnership,* which he wrote in 2010 while he was still Chief Rabbi . . . . Jonathan Sacks tells the story of Judaic beliefs from Abraham's time to the present.

The Mission of Jesus

Jesus himself made few references to these pre-Christian events. His main focus was on interpreting the Mosaic commandments for the new epoch which God wished him to inaugurate. Having lived in obedience to his parents, Mary and Joseph, and having completed his studies to become a Rabbi, he was selected to deliver the usual inauguration address at his local synagogue in Nazareth.

He decided that "The time has come" to announce his mission. He received a mixed reception. Some muttered "is he not just the carpenter's son". For others their hearts told them that he spoke compellingly and with authority. This division was to follow Jesus throughout his short mission.

Jesus, of one mind with God, set out vigorously to fulfil God's will. His mission was to reinstate the authority of the old and most fundamental laws of Judaism, the laws of love, equality, and solidarity. This was to be done by simplifying the excessive complexity and unduly regulated strictness of the existing laws, and restore the care of the poor to its ancient priority. Ref. A 9.

The story of Jesus' public life is beautifully told in the New Testament and in Pope Benedict XV1's book, Jesus *of Nazareth,* 2007.

The Resurrection and Its Aftermath

On the much discussed resurrection, I have always believed in an omnipotent God. My belief in reincarnation leads me to believe that God had to do little bending of the laws of nature for Jesus' soul to ascend to 'His right hand', and to reincarnate recognisably as himself within three days. He could do this with either a spiritual body or a seemingly natural body, depending on the context and occasion. (Ref. Ch 5.). In fact validated case studies indicate that reincarnation may be instantaneous with conception In the case of such a divine re-incarnate it would be inevitable that a very clear message would be sent to the mother, and that many other unusual signs would be seen. This seems to have been the case with Mary.

Jesus' appearances, firstly to his close band of disciples and later to larger numbers, were also within the supernormal category. They were not miracles in the normally understood sense.

In contrast the events that followed them appear to exceed the range of both normal and supernormal events. The first of these events was a decision by his little band of disciples who had been demoralised by the death of Jesus and humiliated by their brutal persecution; suddenly they were filled with zeal, faith, and vigour and set out to undertake the highly dangerous task of preaching his word. Few of them escaped jail and brutalization. More than a few were executed. Still they continued despite continual persecutions for three centuries.

The extent of their extraordinary success is pictured for us by historian Jonathan Kirsh in his 2004 book *God Against the Gods*. His description of Constantine, Emperor of the Western Roman empire and his army, on the point of going into battle against the Emperor of the Eastern Roman Empire is an extraordinary indeed a miraculous contrast.

The sign emblazoned on the shields of Constantine's mobilized troops was the well-known emblem of Christianity.

Weary after their long and urgent march, and badly outnumbered, the omens were not good. Most of the troops were Christians. As he rallied them with his inspiring slogan "Under this sign we will conquer" a great cry went out. They knew they had God on their side. They charged into battle. At its end Constantine was the victorious Emperor of the total Roman Empire, both East and West.

Little wonder that this event has been seen by Christians as the second great miracle which ensued from the Resurrection. In reality it was the culmination of many extraordinary events which attended the apostolic activities of many Christians over those three centuries

How Did the Christians Achieve Such Success

Three hundred years after the little group of disciples set out under Peter's leadership, Christians had reached 10% of the Roman population and were still rising: Such was the appeal to the Roman leadership class of the Christian doctrine of *one true God*, of their style of life ("see how they love one another"), and of their moral authority.

Certain factors that were not of their own making helped. Judaism with its doctrine of one true God appealed to the educated classes in Rome and to many of its political leaders. More Romans would have converted to Judaism but for the requirement of circumcision, conversion on marriage, and   lesser factors such as dietary requirements. These requirements of Judaism outweighed the Christian prohibition on divorce and other lesser requirements.

Against the Christians was their refusal to recognize the Emperor as divine on state occasions. This made them appear as dissidents who could be a threat the state, and was a major cause of many persecutions on the grounds of state security.

On the whole the shrewd Constantine saw that the future lay with the Christians and that Christianity in partnership with himself could best safeguard the stability of the state.

Final Success for Both Christianity and Constantine

To complete the success of the Christians, and of himself, Constantine needed to make one more move. The division within the Christian bishops over the divinity of Christ (Same Substance V Similar Substance) had to be ended.

Constantine called all the Christian bishops, East and West, to a Council. As Kirsch puts it in his book:

'When the bishops marched into the imperial palace at Nicaea in 325, Christianity could still be seen as a radical and subversive movement that set itself against the power and glory of Rome. When they marched out again, however, the bishops had "sealed an alliance of throne and altar" and the church could be regarded as "a branch of the Imperial civil service". . . The Christian church now functioned as "the Christian 'state within a state,'" a kind of shadow government that styled itself after the imperial administration that had once persecuted Christianity. . . . So the apocalyptic visions of the Book of Revelation were now replaced by *realpolitik*'.

After Constantine: The 4th and 5th Centuries.

Constantine's great failure, one so frequently associated with great despots, was that he neglected, or could not bring himself, to lay firm ground on which imperial stability could continue. His sons were not of his calibre. The rest of the 4th century and half of the fifth saw a decline in the quality of imperial decisions: pagans were persecuted by the state.

Eventually the last Emperor was defeated and 'barbarian' kings ruled in Rome and throughout the Empire. Many of these kings were already baptized Christians who had staked out their own dynasties in a selected part of the dying Empire.

The Collapse of the Western Roman Empire

Meanwhile the Western part of the Empire had collapsed under the assaults of 'Barbarian' Kings. Leo, Bishop of Rome, traditionally recognised by all Christian bishops as first amongst equals, had become the *de facto* emperor of the total Roman Empire by the mid 5th century. He became the first Bishop of Rome to be called The Pope. Henceforth the Pope reigned as absolute head over all Western bishops.

Christendom

For the next thousand years, the papacy, with the help of Christian Kings, crushed all heresies, at times with extreme cruelty.

This thousand years was also saw developments in Islamic and Western theology, philosophy, commerce, and science. By 1000CE, religion, philosophy, science and culture had developed to a higher stage in Islam than that prevailing in Christendom.

The Reformation and the Early Enlightenment

In 1517 Martin Luther initiated the Protestant Reformation. He did not question the basic tenets of Genesis. His focus was on the freedom of the individual to use his own conscience in spiritual decisions. He also highlighted the corruption of the Papacy, especially its sale of indulgences.

Efforts to expand Protestantism throughout Europe led to thirty years of war in Europe. Contrary to traditional beliefs, recent historians have shown that these wars were power struggles in which Catholics and Protestants fought on the same side.

The Italian Renaissance, the Reformation, and even the new sciences of the 16th and 17th centuries did not question the basic beliefs of Genesis. Crucially, however, they all opened minds to new concepts of individual dignity. More and more the Popes were seen as immoral, absolutist, and reactionary.

Benedict de Spinoza

The early Enlightenment saw the first challenge to the Papacy with the published writings (1663-77) of Benedict de Spinoza. Spinoza's God is eternal and infinitely perfect. Being a creative and loving God he had no moral choice other than to create our particular universe (Nature).

However, he no longer guides it or us. That he leaves entirely to man. Furthermore he withheld free will, and denied immortality -- beliefs which do not cohere with his own definition of God:

"By God, I understand Being absolutely infinite, that is to say, substance consisting of infinite attributes, each one of which expresses eternal and infinite essence."

(Spinoza *ETHICS*)

There are ambiguous indications in his final book, *The Ethics,* that he was reviewing his beliefs on free will and immortality.

Spinoza's story of creation appealed to scientists and philosophers; it boosted Deism and it led to Atheism. The late Enlightenment following the French Revolution greatly increased this trend.

The leaders of the Christian denominations, but particularly the Papacy, denounced Spinoza as a radical atheist. To escape arrest, trial by the Inquisition and inevitable burning at the stake, Spinoza had to seek refuge in Holland, one of the few liberal states in Europe at the time.

During his lifetime neutral readers of his works saw him as a Deist or a pantheist which is very close to being an atheist. After his death it became increasingly the case that he was seen as a *Panentheist*.

This term describes a person who believes that God is present in every natural thing, but who also believes that the total of all these presences in natural things, does not exhaust God's existence which is a *Supernatural Existence.*

Panentheism is now a substantial religious movement whose core beliefs are very similar to those of Christianity.

The Later Enlightenment

Starting with the Italian Renaissance which was led by Catholics, the Papacy became increasingly anxious as a modernist free-thought movement spread throughout Europe like a slow but inexorable epidemic. The Papacy made a fateful decision to oppose modernism. This decision eventually led to an exodus of intellectuals in the sciences and in the educated classes of the post Industrial Revolution world.

The Success of Science and Technology

The decline of Catholic congregations in the western World was aggravated by increasing household incomes and the development of mass consumption markets. By 1960 a long consumer boom was under way. Happiness on a large scale had arrived. The spiritual messages of an out-of-date Catholic Church were lost in a culture of conspicuous consumption, stoked by industrial advertising and financial instruments which made cheap money available.

Christianity's Capability of Reform and Renewal

However a substantial minority of highly educated people did remain loyal to their churches particularly in the US. The great intellectual resources of Christianity have catered for their need that religion should not contradict reason. St Paul, the early Christian theologians, St. Augustine, Thomas Aquinas, are just a few of the many renowned Christian theologians and philosophers who have enriched western culture. And the great charismatic figures who focused on the poor, such as Jesus and St Francis of Assisi have also had, and still have profound spiritual influence.

Lessons From The USA

Rick Warren is Pastor of Saddleback Evangelical Church, the largest mega-Church in the USA. It claims a congregation of 30,000 believers which is still growing. All comers, whatever their beliefs, get a warm welcome from church volunteers.

His book, *What on Earth Am I Here For – The Purpose Driven Life,* 2012, has sold 30 million copies since its first edition in 2002.

As founding pastor of Saddleback Church Rick Warren leads campuses in major cities around the world. As a theologian, he has lectured at Oxford, Cambridge, University of Judaism, and dozens of universities and seminaries. As a global strategist he advises world leaders and he has spoken to the United Nations, US Congress, Davos Economic Forum. TED, Aspen Institute and numerous Parliaments. He has also founded the global P.E.A.C.E plan which establishes churches of reconciliation, Equips leaders,

Assists the poor, Cares for the sick, and Educates the next generation in 196 countries.

What on Earth Am I Here For is a small and hugely inspiring book. Any Christian who reads it will understand why Evangelical Christianity has been for decades, and still is, the most rapidly growing Christian denomination around the world. I suggest that one big reason for this is the simplicity of its dogmas. To be baptised one need only believe in God and His only son, Jesus. The Evangelical message is that we are here for one purpose and one purpose only: *to worship God and to serve him as Jesus served him.* This message is given with a powerful emotional appeal.

Robert D. Putnam is the Malkin Professor of Public Policy at Harvard University and past president of the American Political Science Association. At the request of their governments he has carried out a number of research projects in different countries on the attitudes of people towards their own religious beliefs. In his own department Putnam has a team of researchers from the necessary disciplines. He also has close co-operative contacts with other eminent Centres of information around the world.

He is renowned for insisting that data be gathered and analysed by the use of the most rigorous statistical methods that are available.

"Who Is A Good American." Americans have long merged patriotism and religion, as evidenced by the vestigial examples of religious symbolism at many moments of nationalist ceremony.

Even though religion and patriotism seemingly fit hand in glove, the 2006 Faith Matters survey reveals that Americans are nonetheless willing to include people who are not religious in their conception of an upstanding citizen. 87% of Americans agree that people "without a religious faith" can be "good Americans" . . . .

Interestingly, this is nearly the same % of Americans (89%) who believe that people of a different faith can go to heaven."

Bridging is the name he gives to the process of having a religiously diverse group of friends and to a society where mixed marriages are seen as normal. Putnam's surveys show that these conditions lead to widening the circle of "we." E pluribus unum.

"How has America solved the puzzle of religious pluralism – the coexistence of religious diversity and devotion? By creating a web of interlocking personal relationships among people of many different faiths. This is America's grace."

Conclusion of Chapter.

This brief examination of salient points in the evolution of Christian beliefs began with Abraham and the advent of Monotheism. The era of the Patriarchs was relatively peaceful, but was still one where conflicts were common. The establishment of monotheism amongst the small Jewish people took two millennia. Nevertheless creative thinking was always active in the great religions that had their roots the Axial Age.

The basic human desire for peace has been continually frustrated. In most eras, and in most nations religious pluralism hasn't even been a pipedream.

In Europe the EU is still an ongoing experiment after half a century, in modern times quite a long period for such a difficult experiment to last. Here, however, the difficulty has not been pluralism between nations but pluralism within nations. It is within nations that an authentic overlapping consensus is most evasive. This is particularly true of the new nations that have been established since the Second World War.

The Catholic Church continued with its reactionary attitude unabated until the advent of Pope John XXIII and the Second Vatican council in the 1960s. He and his successors have won back international respect for the Holy See, but they remained attached to dogma and tradition, and also failed to reform the Curia even when serious scandals within it came to light.

Even more important was their failure to deal with the justified discontents of Catholic women. The result was the loss of many women, and the antagonism of others who remained within the Church.

Yet, while members were lost in Europe, members were gained in South America. Globally, Evangelism has become the fastest growing Christian faith.

The scale of the sexual abuse scandal within the Catholic Church was a most serious blow to its international prestige. Few could have imagined at the beginning of the present millennium that reform and renewal were on the way. This time reform was initiated by theologians and lay people within the Church, not by the hierarchy. (See. Ch 9.)

Chapter 9
The Supernatural Realm.
Trans-communication Between God And Humans.

Introduction
This chapter discusses the means used by a Supernatural God and by his adult human children of the Abrahamic family to speak to one another. The problem is that, compared with what most adult human children know by reason about their parent(s), even His most spiritually aware human children collectively and cumulatively over at least three million years, know very little about their God by reason alone. They don't know how many families He has in our universe who have levels of awareness comparable to his Abrahamic families or his other earthly families. Indeed they don't even know how many universes, or how many unknown categories of awareness, He has created.

God's Direct Communications To Humans
As a believer in the Abrahamic God my understanding of trans-communication between God and humans is as follows. God's *direct* communications to humans are supernatural. Any means that comply with the human level of awareness are available to him. He does not need to use any material instrument of any kind except the human brain. With humans He can choose the most subtle means such as an insightful thought. He can also use an overwhelming revelation as in the case of St. Paul. And there are numerous other means available to Him within the range and outside the range of these two extremes.

A human's ability to receive direct messages from God are proportional to her or his level of spiritual awareness. This is a natural ability which can be supplemented by faith and supernatural grace. Traditionally we believe that modern humans were the first earthly creatures, c. 49,000 years ago, whose brains reached the required level of awareness to receive messages from God. But we earthlings cannot know when God sent the first direct message to earthly creatures. It is argued that it occurred at least 4m.y.a. Because hominins had, by then, the ability to walk upright, they were already accustomed to reading faces. My candidate for God's first significant and direct message to hominins was when the first hominin male and female looked into each other's eyes and felt a dimension in their love that they had not previously felt. Long-term pair bonding followed, leading to family life, kinship bonding, and eventually tribal organisation with the first green shoots of democracy and relevant moral standards.   (Ref. Ch 7.)

God's *Indirect* Ways of 'Speaking' to Humans.

An *indirect* way for God to 'speak' to humans may be another person, or another person's book, or another person's needs. It may be anything in Nature, which is His creation. I believe that His first such indirect message was the Akasha itself, that his second was the ensuing Akashic Field – the Field of Cosmic Consciousness. Both the Akasha and the Akashic Field are part of Nature. He is continuously sending messages. through Nature which embraces all levels of consciousness. What about guardian angels?

Guardian Angels

Yes, I believe in angels. Like every Irish Catholic Child in that era I prayed to my Guardian Angel every morning and every night for a number of years but eventually that good habit ceased, though not my belief in angels. Only very recently have I realized that my neglect of angels was a serious mistake.

Not having been born of humans, angels don't fit in to the Afterworld. Did God create them before the Akasha or were they created together with the Akasha Field? The 200-page paperback *The Physics of Angels, 2014* contains a 57-page dialogue between Matthew Fox and Rupert Sheldrake on this issue. From their research they conclude that the creation of angels simultaneously with the Akasha Field has been the majority view amongst theologians. Almost the entire 57 pages were given to the views of St. Thomas Aquinas who accepted the majority view. I accept Aquinas's views because he studied angels so deeply, and because Laszlo's views cohere so closely to his. Fox and Sheldrake's book contains extensive quotations from his *Summa Theologiae*. Those that are most relevant to my book follow.

Aquinas doesn't use the term 'Field' but he quite clearly has the concept: He talks of angels being localised in a 'place'. . . . .
"It does not follow that an angel is ever contained by a place; for the application to a body of a power of a spiritual substance is, in effect, a containing of the body by that substance and not vice versa. Thus the human soul itself is in the body as containing it and not as contained by it."

There are many analogies in the physical world, such as the gravity field, quantum mechanics, and magnetic fields, where the field does not contain its source.

It is extraordinary how Aquinas's ideas are so close to those of modern quantum theory. They are also expressed in language which is simple and lucid. For that reason I urge readers who have difficulties understanding quantum theory to read this book and then re-read the relevant section in Laszlo's 2014 book.

Fox and Sheldrake's book also discusses Dionysius The Areopagite, and Hildegard of Bingen. Sheldrake's role is to reveal to Fox the convergence of modern Field theory to Aquinas's cosmology.

Rupert: "Aquinas's views fit well with modern field theories.... But the action of angels goes beyond that of souls or fields; it is not an unconscious and habitual part of the course of nature – it involves consciousness or choice."

Matthew: "That is something Aquinas underscores when he says the angel chooses voluntarily to apply its power to a more or less extended body. There's a choice on the part of the angel, a willingness and an option to be creative in this or that 'place' [i.e. Field], connected to these or those bodies."

Angels, in Aquinas's view, are corporeal because they have the power to become embodied and to make themselves seen, like the three strangers who came to Abraham's house in the form of normal human beings. They may do so in modern times. When people say that an angel appeared, they may well be speaking of someone who looked in every way like a normal human being.

Aquinas also says that God alone is non-corporeal but has the power to influence any 'place' he chooses. His 'place' which does not contain Him as He contains it, is absolutely cosmic. It contains all other 'places' including the 'place' of every earthly person and the 'place' of every person in the Afterworld.

Aquinas believed that, as intermediaries between God and humans, angels lived in a spiritual realm of their own; likewise, the Fallen angels also live in a realm of their own where they plan their revenge on God. They too have angelic powers.

The Axial Age.

Millions of years after the hominin enlightenment, the Axial Age (1,000 years b.c.e. to year 1 c.e.) stands out as a period when, it is traditionally believed, many spiritual leaders were directly inspired by God to conceive the fundamental constituents of the Good Life for humans. The Axial Agenda had a promising start, but quickly ran into the sand as militarily-minded empires emerged. (Ref.Ch 7.)

Chapter 8 covers the last two millennia. It shows that during this epoch, spirituality peaked with Jesus and the early church, and that its history has been ambiguous since then, reaching both the most catastrophic and the most divine in the first half of the twentieth century. This chapter deals with the last half century or so and the emergence of new vistas in spirituality.

The New Vistas in Spirituality

By 2013 I had already read and absorbed, as best I could, many of Professor Enda McDonagh's books from the 1960s onwards. I had likewise read and absorbed the latest books of Professor Patrick Masterson and Professor Richard Kearney. (Refs Booklist A).

By 2,013 I was also fully converted to beliefs in authentic near- death experiences, reincarnation, a real creative Afterworld, and Trans-communication between living persons and Afterworld persons, including ITC. I also believed in a Cosmic Consciousness and felt that Laszlo's scientific cosmology was the most coherent and probable of the contemporary scientific proposals. The framework of a possible spiritual cosmology had formed in my mind.

It now remains to revisit my readings of McDonagh, Masterson, Kearney, and others, to discuss their contributions to the new vistas in spirituality, and to see what convergence there is between my ideas and theirs. As all four of us are Catholics there already exists a huge area of convergence in our religious ideas.

Enda McDonagh

As a Professor of Moral Theology, McDonagh's books are rich in theological insights and are written in simple language with a clarity that makes them accessible to laypeople. His teachings on moral philosophy are likewise clear and direct as he summons his reader to examine his or her conscience. He continually draws attention to injustices in Irish political and social life, and in international instances. His spirituality, integrity, empathy, and intellectual resources, are clearly evident and widely recognised.

There are twelve of his books on my shelves, all of which I have read more than once – a number of them repeatedly. There is hardly a topic in theology, philosophy, and related fields which I have met in the writing of other authors that he has not touched on in the twelve books which I have read.

If I have to select one topic with which I have a special affinity it is everyday creativity. I first became aware of his interest in this when he sent me a copy of a lecture he delivered to Maynooth Union Summer School, June, 1962: *Marriage: Source of Life*. In 1975 *Gift and Call,* 189 pages, was published. It was a deep and wide-ranging study of the same topic and had a huge influence on my spiritual formation.

He continued to expand the topic in other books. In 2006 the widely acclaimed *Immersed in Mystery* appeared and included a striking and inspiring theological treatment of everyday creativity and of other important topics.

Enda McDonagh's writings also serve another most important purpose. By opening up critiques of many aspects of Irish Catholic teaching, they have opened the way to new vistas in religion and encouraged a progressive but wise liberalism.

Another major role played by McDonagh is that of the most authoritative critic of the Irish Catholic Hierarchy and of the way it has organised itself in Ireland. Their authoritarian style in dealing with the people of the Church was in sharp contrast with Jesus and the early Christian Church. This he saw as seriously damaging to the development of spirituality in the "whole people of the Church"

He openly criticised the hierarchy for their failures in dealing with the child abuse scandals, and the ensuing cover-ups. The result was that he remained a Professor of Theology. Thus did Irish Catholics loose the benefits of high-level leadership. In the long run they may well gain even more.

Notable is his March 2010 call for a twelve-step reform movement within the Church.

He saw it as an essential step for the Church in healing the results of the child-abuse scandal. The first nine steps are concerned with healing the rift between the abused and the Hierarchy.

The first step says: "All Catholics must remember who the Irish Church is: the whole People of God in Ireland. and that it is the whole People of God under the direction and by the energy of the Holy Spirit who will enable the Church to become a 'recovering' Church".

In the next eight steps he advances a combined top-down and bottom-up approach involving an open dialogue which will include everyone concerned. A series of overlapping meetings should continue until agreement is reached on a way forward. The process should then continue until agreement becomes stabilised. This is a painstaking process, which he expects to take a long time.

[For the full twelve-step program, Google Enda McDonagh]

The last three steps of the programme are concerned with other major long-term problems which concern the future of the Church. They are especially relevant to this book. All three steps are quoted in full.

Step ten: "The intellectual weakness of the Irish Church will also require attention in the path to recovery. Local and national theological 'think tanks' including experts from other disciplines and engaged lay people should be studying and promoting the various needs and possibilities of recovery based on the scriptures, the tradition, doctrines and the history of the Church and the insight of contemporary culture".

Step eleven: "Meantime regular sacramental worship and the practical works of charity and justice, of peace and care for the environment at home and abroad, will continue to strengthen the convalescent church. These activities should include the practices of ecumenism as other Christian Churches come to our aid".

Step twelve: "At some stage the Irish Church as a whole, attentive to the gifts of the spirit which its more localised gatherings have revealed, may be ready for a truly representative assembly. Only in such an assembly can the fruits of the earlier consultations be synthesised and stabilised".

These three steps are an impressive proposal which continues a twofold top-down and bottom-up approach of the previous nine steps. A number of international secular movements have demonstrated that this approach is essential for long term success and stabilisation. It is based on the concept that innate creativity is distributed throughout all normal human populations – a resource that God would surely wish to see fully used.

Patrick Masterson

My introduction to Patrick Masterson's works was his book *Atheism and Alienation*, 1971, which promised another book expanding on the contents of the last Chapter. I eagerly awaited the promised book, but the demands of his ten year Presidency of UCD, followed by his move to The University of Europe, meant that I had to wait until 2001 when The *Sense of Creation was* published.

This book was my introduction to deep and rigorous philosophy – in this case the philosophy of religion. It is written for the interested lay person as well as for the academically tutored person. I found it challenging, spiritually inspiring, and rewarding. It buttressed my belief in the God of Abraham.

It is concerned with philosophical arguments for the existence of such a God. Masterson clarifies a number of basic principles from which such an argument must proceed. He rejects as philosophically inadequate those traditional arguments that assume the existence of a Supreme Being and go on from there to provide the necessary evidence from nature, from revelation, and from the spiritual enrichments that go with such beliefs.

He insists that an argument, which is properly philosophical throughout, cannot have any *a priori* assumptions; argument must begin with basic facts which are accepted as true in normal human discourse. One such fact is that the natural things we perceive around us have their own independent existence; they exist whether or not they are seen by us. If we become aware of them, they may attract us, or we may find them threatening, but unless – as living creatures – they become aware of us, they are not affected by our perceptions. On the other hand, once we become aware of them, both our emotions and our reason are activated.

Our reactions to the things contained in our world are genetically and culturally conditioned over millions of years. Like every animal infant, human infants are initially hard-wired for survival, a task which consumes all of their awareness. This quickly changes, as they begin to identify more 'things' around them: by year two they are connecting things and happenings and developing a vocabulary. If they are fortunate enough to live and be educated in our contemporary developed Western World, most of them will, as adults, have time to think about problems other than survival.

Many of the more educated who are philosophically inclined begin to wonder at the diversity of nature and our universe. How come such a complex entity is so regular in its working, and how did the scientific laws of the universe come about? And, the most difficult question of all, how come our minds are so constructed that they can understand so much about our universe? This last question raises the unresolved problem of human consciousness. In *The Sense of Creation* Masterson confronts it as follows.

"Stated simply, the sequence of physical events in the natural word (i.e., evolution) . . . does not as such explain the existence or nature of our consciousness. In particular it does not explain the openness in virtue of which we transcend our initial first-person-singular perspective on the world and attain an impersonal partial understanding of its objective intelligible structure".

Masterson continues: "The idea that our rational capacity is the product simply of rational selection would leave us no more grounds to trust the results of our reasoning (including the theory of evolution) than if this reasoning were simply the product of our psychological conditioning."

He quotes Aristotle on the issue; "At what moment, and in what manner, do these creatures which have this principle of Reason acquire their share in it, and where does it come from." Aristotle found this a very difficult problem as evolution was not within his philosophical framework. As Masterson puts it: "He [Aristotle] is convinced that 'this difficult' problem is not to be solved by a naturalistic account of our power of reasoning and understanding, It remains then, that Reason alone enters in, as an additional factor, from outside, and that it alone is divine, because physical activity has nothing whatever to do with the activity of Reason [Aristotle]".

A number of naturalistic contemporary philosophers are wrestling with the same problem and have failed to find a resolution even though they know the prevailing facts of evolution and are familiar with contemporary studies of the human mind.

In this context Masterson goes on to quote the naturalistic philosopher Thomas Nagel': "But without something fairly remarkable, human knowledge is unintelligible . . . I believe that unless we suppose that they [our beliefs] have a basis in something global (rather than just human) of which we are not aware, they make no sense – and they do make sense."

Masterson concludes his first argument for the existence of God as follows:

"The foregoing discussion illustrates how an argument for the existence of God can be developed by reflection upon our ability to understand the intelligible structure of the extra-mental world. This intelligibility obtains independently of our limited knowledge which discloses it and which is judged to stand in a non-mutual relationship of real dependence upon it. This paradoxical relationship is a cipher within experience of the analogous relationship of non-mutual real dependence of the world upon God. It serves as a perspicuous source of argument from a "transcendence" manifest within our cognitive experience to the "beyond-experience" absolutely transcendent God".

St.Thomas Aquinas

In his 2012 book, *Approaching God,* Masterson re-develops his second metaphysical argument from his interpretation of the writings of St. Thomas Aquinas:

"For since *esse* is the ultimate source of all perfection of being, God, who as *Esse Subsistence* (self-subsistent unlimited act of existence) possesses the perfection of being in an unlimited or infinite manner all aspects of perfection which characterize being intrinsically [Aquinas]".

The last paragraph restates a key element in the theology of St. Thomas Aquinas whose philosophy underpins Masterson's philosophy of religion. He goes on to present relevant aspects of Aquinas's philosophy. What follows is my selection of passages that are especially relevant to my book

Aquinas: **"The measure of a being's perfection is its degree of *esse*: a being is said to be more or less perfect in proportion to the contraction of its *esse* to a greater or lesser mode of excellence. Hence if there were a being to which the whole perfection of *esse* belonged, no excellence possessed by anything would be lacking to it."** (Aquinas)

Aquinas's definition of God as *Esse Subsistense* provides a necessary extension to Spinoza's definition, as it clarifies the creativity of God as a creativity that is necessarily unceasing, thereby removing a major incoherence in Spinoza's philosophy.

The Theological Approach to God as an Argument For God's Existence

"The theological approach to God and our relationship to him, as distinct from what might be known philosophically, is one which proclaims that the life of God is a life of love and that we have been divinized, have become through grace, part of this life. In the remarkable words of St John: 'And we have come to know, and have believed, the love that God has on our behalf' (1 Jn, 1V, 16)".

(Masterson)

Masterson claims that in view of the other components involved – intellect and will – the faith of the believer is affirmed as an intellectually justifiable, reliably motivated, and freely sustained commitment to God's revelation accepted as such.

It does involve attending to the historical evidence of God's revelation provided by the objective experience and teaching of examples of great holiness and prophetic witness to God –

holiness and witness most evidently and perfectly manifested and exemplified in the life of Jesus.

Masterson and Phenomenology

Phenomenology is a very complex concept which has engaged a number of leading philosophers since the early 20th century, including Husserl, Heidegger, and Merleau-Ponty. None of them have quite the same view. My simplistic short answer to the question 'What is the phenomenal approach to God?' is as follows:

Continuing from the last paragraph of page eight:

Phenomenologists believe that, using appropriate psychological methods, a person can get to a mature *unconditioned mind* by bracketing all normal thinking, events, etc., and putting them to one side. In such a state a person can have a unique communication directly from God, if her or his mind is sufficiently open to God through prayer and other religious practices. For some gifted individuals and on some occasions, the direct experience of God is so overwhelming or *Saturating* that they feel almost face to face with God without any intermediary.

Readers unacquainted with the Phenomenological Approach to God should read Richard Kearney's masterly exposition in his 2010 book, *Anatheism,* which preceded Masterson's 2010 book by two years.

What follows is a critique by Masterson, in his 2012 book, of the phenomenal approach to God:

"Is it the transcendent God himself who is given in our experiential sense of God? Or is it an effect or cipher of his transcendent reality which must be deciphered metaphysically? Or is it perhaps only an hallucination or illusion? In other words, beyond the *assertability conditions* of the affirmed experience, there remains the issue of the *theoretical truth conditions* which must obtain if the assertion of the experience is to be more than just that – however sincere or convinced. It seems to me that this further question, in effect a metaphysical issue, is not only legitimate but also necessary. It seems unreasonable not to look for an ultimate explanation of how an allegedly dependable and irreducible experience of divine transcendence is possible. If we seek theoretical explanations even of unproblematic 'natural' experiences, surely it is reasonable to look for an explanation of a 'saturating' experience which exceeds our constitutive capacity and comprehension". Masterson continues,

"There is a tension, if not a downright contradiction, inherent in any phenomenological assertion of an experience of divine transcendence as both unconditional and also as co-relative to human subjectivity, a finite subjectivity however graciously transformed. This tension can be mitigated and perhaps even resolved by considering it in a wider metaphysical context. In such a context the phenomenological indication of divine transcendence is appraised as an experienced finite cipher, trace, saturated impression or effect of an ontologically independent *non-experienced* God. . . . . In such a mediated indirect affirmation of divine transcendence, God can indeed be said unproblematically to be the origin of our 'sense of God'".

I find Patrick Masterson arguments for the existence of God convincing and spiritually inspiring. He proposes them as arguments, not as proofs. He accepts that religiosts are more likely than naturalists to be convinced. As rational philosophical arguments they permit a dialogue between believers and non-believers – a dialogue which open-minded non-believers cannot reasonably ignore. Therefore arguments such as his are, as he says, essential in protecting and advancing core philosophical beliefs in a transcendent God. Such metaphysical arguments must therefore continue. There is not now, nor is there likely to be an 'after metaphysics'.

I am aware of one important theological point where I diverge from Professor Masterson. I believe that an altruistic God would feel morally obliged to relinquish His powers of constraint over the freedom of his adult human children. On that point I am closer to the position of Richard Kearney. I am sure that Professor Masterson would have reservations about a number of my other beliefs. I hope for the privilege of his critique.

Richard Kearney

Because I found both his thinking and his writing style exhilarating, I have been a fan of Richard Kearney for decades. His recent books, which are very relevant to this book, are more than exhilarating. This reader was spiritually moved by Kearney's deep personal commitment to the Abrahamic God and to the teachings of Jesus, based on his studies of the Bible.

The God Who May Be, 2000.

In this book he tells of how his studies of the Old Testament together with his vast knowledge of new trends in Christian thinking, brought him to the belief that the Jewish interpretation of the Old Testament was more correct than the prevailing Christian interpretation, on one most important point.

He writes: "Interpretations of the conventional English translation "I am who am" or "I am he who is" can be met with a powerful counter-tradition – "I shall be what I shall be" [Jewish Bible]. He follows this by describing the Exodus exchange between God and Moses as "a still small voice that whispers and cries in the wilderness: *perhaps . . . I am who may be if you continue to keep my word and struggle for the coming of justice"*.

Throughout his book, Kearney sustains this theme of God needing the help of his human creatures if He is to become complete, and he develops it further in his 2010 book *Anatheism*, where he agrees with other European philosophers, that *kenosis* (or empting out) can be applied not only to Jesus, but also to God. Readers of my book will note that one of its central concepts is that a loving and creative God would feel obliged to forego, or 'empty Himself of his power' to constrain his human children, if he wished them to have full freedom to choose either good or evil.

Atheistic Criticism of Monotheism

Kearney accepts that Enlightenment atheists have ample evidence that monotheism has been an "irremediable   source of intolerance and war". But he says that on "the other hand, the Abrahamic legacy provides powerful resources for those – like this author – who wish to retrieve a liberating message in the Bible, one that fosters radical attentiveness to the stranger as portal to the sacred".

The Anatheist Wager

Kearney explains his complex idea of anatheism thus: "The anatheist wager I am trying to describe has five main components: *Imagination, humour, commitment, discernment, and hospitality.* .
. . .   In sum, I am wagering on the possibility of a spiritual acoustics capable of reinterpreting the oldest cries of the religious heart in both our sacred and secular worlds. But to open oneself to such radical attention one must, I suggest, abandon the old God of sovereignty and theodicy. That Master God must die so that the God of interconfessional hospitality can be born. And, in so far as religious dogma has often served as a vehicle of infantile fear and dependency, the interreligious God may be described as a post dogmatic God. That is why anatheism appreciates a rigorous atheistic critique of the theistic perversions of religion, . . ."

Kenosis

Turning to the concept of *Kenosis* (or emptying out), Kearney goes on: "Another aspect of the fivefold wager . . . . is the *powerlessness* of the divine. Revisiting previous thinking has led to a focus on the notion of Incarnation as *kenosis*. By this I understand the self-emptying of the omnipotent God, the surpassing of metaphysical categories of divinity as First Cause or Highest Being, the realization that God is a promise, a call, a desire to love and be loved that cannot *be* at all unless we allow God to be God."

(Kearney)

The Secularization of Religion

Kearney admires a number of prominent writers who, from the 1940s to the present time have seen that the best hope for the survival of religion is its secularisation -- God without religion. He writes of leading figures such as *Bonhoeffer, Ricoeur,* and other European thinkers:

"A short time before his execution, as the shadow of death crossed his prison walls, he (Bonhoeffer) wrote this poignant last testament: 'I have come to understand more and more the profound this-worldliness of Christianity. The Christian is not a *homo religiousus,* but simply a man, as Jesus was a man . . . . I don't mean the shallow and banal this-worldliness of the enlightened, the busy, the comfortable, or the lascivious, but the profound this-worldliness, characterized by discipline and constant knowledge of death and resurrection . . . It is only by living completely in this world that one learns to have faith . . . By this-worldliness I mean living unreservedly in life's duties, problems, successes, experiences and perplexities, In so doing we throw ourselves completely into the arms of God, taking seriously, not our own sufferings, but those of God and the world – watching with Christ in Gethsemane'".

Ricoeur's Post-religious Faith:

"Perhaps the contemporary philosopher who most consistently pursued Bonhoeffer's notion of postreligious faith was Paul Ricouer. A fellow prisoner in a Nazi camp, he managed to survive. Ricoeur spoke of faith as "the joy of yes in the sadness of no." He famously described his own Protestant faith as a "chance converted into destiny by a constant choice." Nothing about God could be taken for granted. On the contrary, having lived for five years in German captivity during the war, Ricoeur knew there could be no return to faith that did not fully acknowledge the traversal of the abyss. He also recognized that the trenchant critiques of religion, delivered by atheists like Freud, Marx, and Nietzsche, had to be taken seriously".

(Kearney)

Kearney continues: "The sacramental moment of anatheism is when we finally restore the hyphen between the secular and the sacred. It is also the moment we return from text to action, from the realm of critical interpretation to the world of quotidian praxis and transformation. This ultimate transition from word to flesh is witnessed daily wherever someone gives a cup of cold water to a thirsting stranger. For in such situations one's faith in God as stranger is not a matter of theories or ideas but of living witness to the word made flesh. There are countless examples of this at every border, street corner, or threshold where a native meets a foreigner and opens the door to the messiah in our midst.

I am not suggesting that faith is only genuine if it has passed through the grids of Western liberal secularism.

Far from it: the faith that anatheism gestures toward has always been there, in past ages, and in non-Western cultures and societies too. It was there wherever a person suspended her certainty about a familiar God and opened the door to the stranger. And, we may ask, was there any religion anywhere on earth that did not witness such gestures of hospitality? Anatheism is not something that comes only at the end of history, as dialectical teleologies might suggest. It marks the eternal crossing of time. It was there from the beginning and recurs at every moment that the stranger trumps the sovereign". (**Kearney**)

"Anatheism does not propose a new God, a new belief, a new religion. It simply invites us to see what has always been there *a second time around –ana"* (**Kearney**)

Particularly in this chapter I realise that I have been using a very crude brush in trying to present the thoughts of three major writers in fifteen or so pages. Presenting selected passages, which are judged to be most relevant to my own book, inevitably distorts the carefully judged balance of their books. Even worse, I am far from confident that their thoughts have not been misrepresented. I can only plead for forgiveness from all three writers and rely on their empathetic tolerance with a self-taught philosopher.

The New Religious Vistas: A Summary
Chapter 8 covered the negative attitude of the Catholic Church in Ireland to new religious vistas that emerged in the post-World War Two period. Despite that, new religious vistas, cautiously but firmly, began to emerge in Ireland from within the Catholic Church.

The omens were not propitious for reform. The authoritarian process which the Hierarchy had exercised so effectively in the mission they were given of civilizing and educating the Irish, had run its course by the end of the nineteenth century. But it had become deeply rooted in the psychology of the clergy, and was given almost a free reign by successive Irish governments until the late twentieth century. On questions of morality their decisions continued to hold sway until recent referenda indicated that opposition to their wishes was no longer electorally disastrous.

History will show that, over the last half century, Enda McDonagh was the leading reformer within the Irish Catholic Church. He was denied the promotions which would have given the whole people of the Church in Ireland the spiritual and intellectual leadership they needed, but he was not sanctioned.

It says a lot about the esteem in which he was held by many bishops, that they would discuss contentious issues with him in a warm friendly way. He was able to speak more and more trenchantly in his call for reform. His twelve point plan for the Irish Catholic Church will remain a call that must inevitably prevail. It will take just one senior bishop to openly initiate such a plan in his diocese. Popular support would be immense. It must be kept in mind that all Catholic bishops were under immense pressure from a conservative Papacy and Curia, to toe the Papal line.

It is to be hoped that Patrick Masterson will produce more books which will demonstrate that metaphysical arguments will remain essential well into the future.

Richard Kearney's spiritual commitment and fertile mind will continue to open, and revise, new vistas in spirituality.

Conclusion

As already mentioned, there is inevitably a huge convergence of ideas between all contemporary Christian thinkers on religious questions – if the question of new scientific vistas are excluded. As of now, Keith Ward remains the only leading theologian to show a tentative interest in reinterpreting the Genesis story in a way that takes account of what is now scientific knowledge of the higher levels of awareness that can be reached after death by everyone of goodwill.

I look forward to theologians and philosophers of religion now turning their thoughts to the new scientific information on the Afterworld and seriously exploring the spiritual benefits that may be harvested from the new vistas in science. The existing theology of life after death, "the Communion of Saints, the forgiveness of sins and the resurrection of the body", is woefully inadequate.

A spiritual cosmology such as that advanced in this book by Ervin Laszlo or by myself can only be a tentative one until it has been subjected to a thorough theological and metaphysical analysis. When that is done a more comprehensive cosmology will be the result and that will itself be superseded as new insights emerge in theology, philosophy, psychology, metaphysics, and science.

A succession of greater levels of awareness is how God has communicated most comprehensively with His human children in the past. No one knows what God has in mind. We await His will.

Chapter 10
The Role of Secular Agencies

Introduction

At present there are a wide range of secular agencies who see themselves engaged in the broad task of long-run human development. Some are governmental agencies whose financial resources are provided by government. Many are Non-governmental agencies (NGOs) who are financed by the private sector. Very many are mixtures of these two categories and enjoy support from both public and private sectors. They are regulated by the UN and usually operate with a high degree of autonomy. Full lists may be found on the internet.

In this chapter three selected world-wide agencies will be briefly described, and their convergence with spiritual approaches discussed.

The Capabilies Approach (CA) to Human Development

Introduction

There are a number of UN-approved versions of the CA being practiced with Governmental approval. Dr. Amartya Sen, a world class Indian economist, is seen as the father of this approach. Working in India he identified a List of Central Capabalities (LCC) that a person must have if he or she is to have a life of dignity. His work caught the attention of Professor Martha Nussbaum who worked with him and eventually developed her own List of Central Capabilities (LCC) with his approval.

I have selected her particular approach for description in this Chapter. Her 2010 book, *The Capabilities Approach,* gives a full account of her own LCC. The book was written for students and interested laypeople. It is highly recommended reading. What follows are based on selected passages.

A Capabilities Approach

Improving people's quality of life requires wise policy choices and dedicated action on the part of many individuals. The Capabilities Approach sets out to be an alternative to the GDP approach [Gross Domestic Product, a purely economic measure of overall national production and average production per capita.] that would incorporate important social values.

The Capabilities Approach has typically been elaborated in the context of international development policy, with a focus on poorer nations that are struggling to improve their quality of life. More recently, richer nations have compiled their own Human Development Reports, and their data have always been important in the Reports of the United Nations [UN] Human Development Reports Office. Still, the approach is sometimes thought of as suited only to poorer countries.

All nations, however, contain struggles for lives worthy of human dignity, and all contain struggles for equality and justice. This would be found less often in countries with higher rates of literacy, but these often fail to deliver functional literacy to their students, and at higher levels of education alarming inequalities in access remain. Domestic violence and inequalities in health care and nutrition are also common in rich countries. For all then, the Capabilities Approach supplies insight.

Ten Central Capabilities

Considering the various areas of human life in which people move and act, this approach to social justice asks, What does a life worthy of human dignity require? At a bare minimum, an ample threshold level of ten Central Capabilities is required. Given a widely shared understanding of the task of government (namely, that government has the job of making people able to pursue a dignified and minimally flourishing life), it follows that a decent political order must secure to all citizens at least a threshold level of these ten Central Capabilities:

1. Life. Being able to live to the end of a human life of normal length; not dying prematurely, or before one's life is so reduced as to be not worth living.

2. Bodily health. Being able to have good health, including reproductive health; to be adequately nourished, to have adequate shelter.

3. Bodily integrity. Being able to move freely from place to place; to be secure against violent assault, including sexual assault and domestic violence; having opportunities of sexual satisfaction and for choice in matters of reproduction.

4. Senses, imagination and thought. Being able to use the senses, to imagine, think, and reason – and to do these things in a "truly human" way, a way informed and cultivated by an adequate education, including, but by no means limited to, literacy and basic mathematical and scientific training. Being able to use imagination and thought in connection with experiencing and producing works and events of one's choice, religious, literary, musical, and so forth. Being able to use one's mind in ways protected by guarantees of freedom of expression with respect to both political and artistic speech, and freedom of religious exercise. Being able to have pleasurable experiences and to avoid nonbeneficial pain.

5. Emotions. Being able to have attachments to things and people outside ourselves; to love those who love and care for us, to grieve at their absence; in general, to love, to grieve, to experience longing, gratitude, and justified anger. Not having one's emotional development blighted by fear and anxiety. (Supporting this capability means supporting forms of human associations that can be shown to be crucial in their development.)

6. *Practical reason.* Being able to form a conception of the good and to engage in critical reflection about the planning of one's life. (This entails protection for the liberty of conscience and religious observance.)

7. *Affiliation. (A)* Being able to live with and toward others, to recognize and show concern for other human beings, to engage in various forms of social interaction; to be able to imagine the situation of another. (Protecting this capability means protecting institutions that constitute and nourish such forms of affiliation, and also protecting the freedom of assembly and political speech.) *(B)* Having the social bases of self-respect and nonhumiliation; being able to be treated as a dignified being whose worth is equal to that of others. This entails provisions of non-discrimination on the basis of race, sex, sexual orientation, ethnicity, caste, religion, national origin.

8. *Other species.* Being able to live with concern for and in relation to animals, plants, and the world of nature.

9. *Play.* Being able to laugh, to play, to enjoy recreational activities.

10. *Control over one's environment.*

(A) Political. Being able to participate effectively in political choices that govern one's life; having the right of political participation, protection of free speech and association.

(B) Material. Being able to hold property (both land and movable goods), and having property rights on an equal basis with others; having the right to seek employment on an equal basis with others; having the freedom from unwarranted search and seizure. In work, being able to work as a human being, exercising practical reason and entering into meaningful relationships of mutual recognition with other workers.

Capabilities belong first and foremost to individual persons, and only derivatively to groups. The CA stipulates that the goal is to produce capabilities for each and every person.

Developing and elaborating the List of Central Capabilities (LCC) will remain a work-in-progress. There are now many advisory Consultants operating in this field with Governmental Approval. Some are followers of Nussbaum and Sen; others have developed their own UN-approved LCCs.

Practitioners in the CPA approach adopt the bottom-up principle that implementation can be successful only if the people on the ground are supportive and are given every opportunity of using their personal creativity. This is done by organising a system of group discussions in which everyone is involved and encouraged to express their ideas. This approach in itself is now widely recognized as a major element in developing the capabilities of all involved.

Advisory consultants avoid situations where the conditions do not exist that are necessary for use of the bottom-up approach.

Bottom-up approaches have been developed in many fields, including the field of psychology, as described by Geraldine Moane in her book Gender and Colonialism. In her book she outlines the reasons why bottom-up approaches are so important in bringing about change. This approach holds even if there is hostility from the top.

Human Development: National Health Issues
Introduction

This example of the role of secular movements in human development has striking parallels to the CA approach: it, too, sees the bottom-up approach as essential for successful implementation. It differs in that governments provide full financing. It also differs in that it has been initiated in the developed world and has become a key policy issue in the EU.

That body plans to establish long-term EU-wide standards in the implementation process, and has already taken steps in that direction.

However, EU countries vary in the progress they have already made in dealing with the problems of mental ill-health. In most of them books describing their approach to problems have been published.

In 2014 Dr. Peter Kinderman published *The New Laws of Psychology* which gives an excellent account of the British experience and its involvement with the EU. The British Health Services lag behind the better EU countries and the Irish Health Services lag even further behind. As many of our problems are similar to those in Britain I have selected Dr. Kinderman's book as an example of the thinking underlying future goals in the EU. He writes as follows.

Biological Determinism

Biological explanations for complex human phenomena are common and powerful. The neurotransmitter dopamine (which has been linked to many street drugs and to psychosis) seems to have a role in making events seem more personally significant and salient, and has been linked to a range of mental-health problems, including psychotic experiences such as hallucinations and persecutory delusions. Serotonin (another neurotransmitter) has been linked to mechanisms of reward and social status, and therefore to depression and low self-esteem.

Biological accounts are important and useful, since human life cannot be fully understood unless the working of the human brain is understood. However, neuroscience without psychology is unlikely to explain why two people are different. Understanding the psychology of how people make sense of their world is necessary for understanding human behaviour and emotions, and therefore mental health problems.

Social Determinism

We are immersed in societies that form, support and mould us. In part, we behave as we do because of the social circumstance in which we find ourselves. We are, in part, the product of the rewards and punishments that we have received throughout our life. All this is true but it still may be inadequate to explain differences in how people behave, because it is also true that different people respond to and make sense of similar life experiences in different ways.

Making Sense of the World

People are more than mere biological machines and are more than unthinking clay, moulded by social and circumstantial pressures. We make sense of our world. Our beliefs, emotions and behaviours – including our mental health – are the product of the way we think about ourselves, other people, the world and the future.

These thoughts are, in turn, the consequence of our learning: the social circumstances, life events and experiences that we have been exposed to and the ways in which we have understood and responded to them. Our brain is a supremely efficient machine for learning, and we make sense of our experiences.

In our human lives most things are done for very straightforward reasons – people make sense of their world and act accordingly. We can use this knowledge to understand not only mental health but also other key aspects of our lives – relationships, families, work, happiness, moral decisions.

Learning:

Human beings are born as natural learning engines. To develop the adult vocabulary of 20,000 words, children have to be able to learn up to 20 new words a day. This learning is best understood as the development of mental models of the world. These models are complex, and often largely unconscious, constructions that depend on the simultaneous manipulation of abstract representations of the world.

To make sense of the world, we have to construct abstract representations of the world, and are constantly processing information on many levels simultaneously. So, our mental models of the world are built up from the simultaneous manipulation of enormous numbers of complex abstract representations of the world. These models have enormous significance, as they explain how people think, feel, and behave.

This suggests that, although we do differ at birth, these differences have much more to do with the different experiences and cultures to which we have been exposed. This makes neuroscience a servant of psychology, not the other way around.

We build up our picture of the world from the evidence of our senses, rather than 'seeing' an image of the world projected onto our brains. This means we make a lot of mistakes, and much of our picture of the world is a –very effective – 'best guess'.

What we think we see might not always fully reflect the objective reality, and this applies particularly to psychological distress. People become depressed or anxious because of their negative thoughts about themselves, other people, the world and the future.

In very distressing cases, people can become deluded and can hallucinate. They can be certain they are being persecuted and that they can hear disembodied voices. . . . these distressing beliefs can be mistaken. Even our sense of self is a construction. We understand who we are and how we function by making working models of ourselves in our minds – and its these working models we need to understand.

This means that many mental-health illnesses – paranoia, depression, social anxiety, etc. – may be the result of poor learning experiences rather than biological deficits.

Unlike other animals we use complex, abstract concepts such as 'trust', or 'love' and manipulate these abstractions. These matter because they have important consequences. People behave differently because trust is degraded. Many of our most important behaviours, especially in relationship, are shaped in part by these complex and abstract ways of understanding our social world.

Of course this is hugely complicated, so that much of our day-to-day human thought is based on simple rules of thumb and rapid practically useful near-guesses.

The New Laws of Psychology

Kinderman: 'I believe it's now possible to summarise all these [modern psychological ideas that we have looked at] in two new laws of psychology:

Law 1. Our thoughts, emotions and behaviour (and therefore out mental health and well being) are largely determined by how we make sense of the world.

Law 2. How we make sense of the world is largely determined by our experiences and upbringing.

Well-being

As in physical health, where the role of the physician is now actively to promote health, not merely to treat illnesses, so it is in psychiatry. The role of psychiatry is increasingly focussing on the promotion of mental health – even the promotion of positive mental well-being.

The present UK government's strategy for mental health, launched in 2011, stresses the breadth and prevalence of mental health problems in the general population, with perhaps one person in every four personally experiencing psychological problems in their lifetime. And, as a government strategy should, it stresses the cost to the economy of mental health problems – at least £77 billion each year and possibly as much as £105 billion.

It comments that a million people in the UK are receiving incapacity benefit, with 40% of these off work because of mental health problems; that a third of GP consultations are estimated to be a result of mental health issues; and that such problems constitute the largest proportion of 'disease burden' in public health. Finally, it discusses the disturbingly higher proportion of early deaths in people with mental health problems.

The European Commission takes a step further, describing mental health as: a resource which enables people to realize their intellectual and emotional potential and to find and fulfil their roles in social, school and working life. For societies good mental health of citizens contributes to prosperity, solidarity and social justice. The commission also suggests that: 'the mental condition of people is determined by a multiplicity of factors.'

Mental Capital In 2008, the United Kingdom's Government office for Science, under the Chief Scientific Adviser, Sir David King and his successor, Sir John Babington, commissioned the Foresight Project on Mental Capital and Wellbeing. The ambitious aim was to review the best available scientific evidence influencing our mental development and well-being from conception until death. The authors of the report were able to recruit over 400 leading international scientific experts to contribute to the report. These were drawn from a range of disciplines including neuroscience, psychology and psychiatry, economics, genetics, social sciences and education.

The resulting Forecast Report defined 'mental capital' as 'the totality of an individual's cognitive and emotional resources, including their cognitive capability, flexibility and efficiency of learning, emotional intelligence (e.g. empathy and social cognition), and resilience in the face of stress. The extent of an individual's resources reflects his/her basic endowments (genes and early biological programming), and their experience and education, which takes place throughout the lifecourse'. The authors also defined 'mental well-being' as 'a dynamic state in which the individual is able to develop their potential, work productively and creatively, build strong and positive relationships with others, and contribute to their community. It is enhanced when an individual is able to fulfil their personal and social goals and achieve a sense of purpose in society'.

Measuring Well-Being

The UK Office for National Statistics have been given the difficult job of reaching a UK consensus on measuring well-being which covers such a wide range of issues: relationships, mental health, physical health, physical security, quality and security of our housing, nature and quality of employment, access to and appreciation of opportunities in the areas both of sports and leisure, and arts and culture. Spirituality and religious life is extremely important to some people, a sense of meaning and purpose in society and democratic political participation. It's clear that we are talking about a spectrum of wellbeing in all these areas, for example in mental well-being, not a distinction between 'well' and 'ill'.

The Flourishing Movement: Its Role in Human Development.

Introduction

Two excellent books on Flourishing are:
Dr. Martin Seligman's book, Flourish, 2011 and
Dr. Maureen Gaffney's book, Flourishing, 2011.

Dr. Martin Seligman is a leading figure in the Flourishing movement. He is Professor of Psychology at the University of

Pennsylania and former president of the American Psychological Association. When he was elected President he initiated university programmes in Positive Psychology, and was engaged by the US Armed Forces to organize courses for soldiers at all levels. He is likewise engaged by a number of major international industrial organisations, and by a number of countries as an adviser.

Dr. Maureen Gaffney is Adjunct Professor of Psychology and Society at University College Dublin. Over the past ten years she has divided her time between consultancy and a number of State and other Boards. She has served as chair of the National Economic and Social Forum, board member of the Health Service Executive, and council member of the Economic and Social Research Institute.

Dr. Seligman
What Is Well-Being?

According to Dr. Seligman: Each element of well-being must itself have three properties to count as an element: 1. It contributes to well-being. 2. Many people pursue it for its own sake, not merely to get any of the other elements. 3. It is defined and measured independently of the other elements (exclusively)

Well-being theory has five elements, and each of the five has the above three properties:

1. Positive emotion
2. Engagement [or flow]
3. Meaning (belonging to and serving something that you believe is bigger than the self)
4. Accomplishment
5. Positive relationships

1 and 2 are assessed only subjectively. 3 is not solely a subjective state. The dispassionate and more objective judgment of history,

logic, and coherence can contradict a subjective judgment. 4. May not be for everyone. 5. Very little that is positive is solitary.

Young People and Well-Being
Depression now ravages teenagers: fifty years ago, the average age of the first onset was about thirty. Now the first onset is below age fifteen . . . . all of us in the field are dismayed by how much depression there is now and how most of it goes untreated.

Thought, focusing, planning and inhibiting fast impulsive thoughts are not the only important slow processes. Creativity is surely one. Deciding which of alternative paths to take we call planning . . . .beyond this, the invention of new paths captures much of what is meant by creativity.

Self-discipline outpredicts IQ for academic success by a factor of about 2, and probably explains why girls do better at second level. IQ tests show no difference in IQ

Women's superior self-control does not wane with maturity, but after college many are swamped by cultural factors that dampen the female self-discipline edge.

The shape of genius – with the top performers outdistancing the average excellent performer by a much greater margin than they would in bell-shaped distributions – follows from multiplying, rather than adding, the underlying causes of genius. . . This is the underlying rationale for GRIT, the never-yielding form of self-discipline.

Controlling for education, older people have more GRIT than younger people with those over sixty-five having much more than any other age group.

Comprehensive Soldier Fitness
The army has decided that it indeed wants its soldiers to answer to a higher moral order. So that by strengthening soldiers' moral and

ethical values, the army's operations – which presents knotty moral dilemmas frequently – will be carried out ethically

1.   There is considerable evidence that a higher level of spirituality goes hand in hand with greater well-being, less mental illness, less substance abuse, and more stable marriages, not to mention better military performance – an advantage that is particularly salient in facing major adversity such as combat.

In this module, spiritual fitness is not theological but human. It takes no stand on the validity of religious or secular frameworks. Rather it supports and encourages a soldier to search for truth, self-knowledge, right action, and purpose in life: living by a code that is rooted in belonging to and serving something he believes is larger than the self.

The module focuses on the soldiers "spiritual core," consisting of self-awareness, sense of agency, self-regulation, self-motivation, and social awareness.

Positive Physical Health
It is all too common not to be mentally ill but to be stuck and languishing in life. Positive mental health is a presence: of positive emotion, of engagement, of meaning, of good relationships, of accomplishment. It is not merely being disorder free; rather it is the presence of flourishing.

History and Progress
Dr. Seligman writes: I believe that history is the account of human progress and that you have to be blinded by ideology not to see the reality of this progress. With fits and starts, the moral and economic envelope of recorded is, nevertheless, upward. As a child of the Great Depression and the Holocaust, I am clear eyed about the terrible obstacles that remain. I am clear eyed about the fragility of prosperity, and of the billions of human beings who do not yet enjoy the flowers of human progress. But it cannot be

denied that even in the twentieth century, the bloodiest of all our centuries, we defeated fascism and communism, we learned how to feed six billion people, and we created universal education and universal medical care. We raised real purchasing power more than fivefold. We extended the lifespan. We began to curb pollution and care for the planet, and we made huge inroads into racial, sexual, and ethnic injustice. The age of the tyrant is coming to an end, and the age of democracy has taken firm root.

These economic, military, and moral victories are our proud heritage of the twentieth century. What gift will the twenty-first century pass to our prosperity?

More than just measuring flourishing, our gift will be more flourishing itself. I underscore the downstream benefits of flourishing. Much of this book has been about these downstream effects: when individuals flourish, health, productivity, and peace follow. With this in mind, I now articulate the long mission for positive psychology.

By the year 2051, 51% of the people of the world will be flourishing.

The very first positive psychology congresses took place in China and India in August 2010. I cannot foresee [what will happen in Asia], but I am mindful of contagion: happiness turns out to be more contagious than depression, and upward spirals around positive goals will occur.

Dr. Gaffney, Flourishing

Dr. Gaffney writes about Flourishing: Teams and organisations also have a 'mental life'. Most leaders work hard to get alignment – getting everybody on the same *thinking* wavelength. But to help organisations and teams to flourish, leaders must also work equally hard on getting attunement – getting people on the same *feeling* wavelength, getting the purpose of the organization and the meaning of the work to resonate with people in a felt way. 'Felt' is the important word here. Leaders of flourishing organisations succeed in making strong feeling connections between the personal goals of values of the people working there and those of the organisation, or even the larger society. The tighter the links in the chain, the happier the people and the better this results.

Paul Baltes: Wisdom . . . . is about understanding the 'fundamental pragmatics of life', being able to link the lessons you have learned from very different domains in life; knowing something about the essence of the human condition and the ways to best manage it. It is a rich mix of practical experience; of insight about how people behave; of tolerance of other people and their opinions (mainly as a result of learning from your own mistakes); of recognizing the inherent complexity and uncertainty in life. It is recognising the limits of your ability to understand and predict things and still being able to positively manage the uncertainty.

New research is showing that there is a remarkable similarity between the dynamics of individual and organizational flourishing. First, to flourish, people need to make a connection between the practical things they are doing and some deeper value that motivates them. So, too with organizations. Organizational values such as compassion, gratitude, forgiveness, internal trust and optimism may seem remote from profitability, productivity, quality, customer retention. Research shows that those who score higher on such values perform significantly better than other organizations on precisely those practical things. Having a sense of goodness is just as important for organizations as for individuals.

Yet another study of 198,000 employees across nearly 8,000 organizations globally found that only 20% of people felt that they had the opportunity to do what they do best every day.

This is an extraordinary loss of happiness and a waste of human potential, not just for the individuals themselves, but for society at large.

Positive breeds positivity: Barbara Fredrickson, the leading researcher on positive emotions, identifies ten major positive emotions. Listed in the order in which we most frequently experience them they are:

1. love
2. joy
3. gratitude
4. contentment
5. interest
6. hope
7. pride
8. amusement
9. inspiration
10. awe

What they share is this: they trigger the urge to engage with life, become pleasurably absorbed in experience, to be open, receptive and alert to possibilities.

Knowing who you really are

Innate drives: Paul Lawrence and Nitin Nohria of Harvard University propose four:

1. The drive to **defend** ourselves, those we love, what we own, what we believe in and what we value.

2. The drive to **acquire** objects and experiences that improve our status relative to other people, what we might loosely call a drive to achieve or compete.

3. The drive to **bond** in long-term relationships of mutual care and commitment, is social groups for pleasure and company, in networks of cooperation to secure resources and get things done.

4. The drive to **learn** and make sense of the world and of ourselves, to master things, to experiment, to innovate and create.

The Higher Self

This realm of the Self is the hardest to describe. It is unconscious to the extent that we are normally very preoccupied by the demands of surviving and managing our lives, so we lose sight of this highest part of our consciousness. Yet, intuitively we know it is there. It is where our capacity for imagination, creativity and spirituality resides, where we feel connected to some bigger force outside ourselves and know that we are more than just how our past circumstances define us. . . . Poets, writers and artists and artists of all kinds are usually very connected to their higher self because they draw their creative energy from there.

This is also where your highest values and character strengths reside: your capacity for wisdom; for courage; for love; for justice and leadership; for forgiveness and integrity; for faith, hope and purpose. These are the character strengths that most of us would like to be described as possessing, and would like to instil in our children. They constitute a vital part of flourishing – not just in our individual lives, but in organizations, communities and society.

This higher realm of yourself is where you bring unity and coherence into your sense of self. Hovering half within and half outside consciousness is your need for identity, for purpose and meaning in your life. You need to feel that you are somebody and that your life matters.

Much of this psychological work is done through creating a life narrative. Your overall narrative of 'who I am' is a combination of the story you tell yourself about yourself, the stories that important others tell you about you, and the stories you act out in your life. This life narrative can be profoundly shaken by setbacks, and by loss. But, most importantly, it can also be rewritten in a way that helps you flourish under fire. One of the most powerful ways that narrative can be reshaped is through your capacity to reflect and to imagine – which happens at the higher level of self.

Dr. Gaffney concludes:

Happy people have better health and live longer; they have more friends and better relationships;

What do they do to produce such good outcomes? They seek out other people; they are helpful to others; they look on the bright side of life and have resilience when the negatives arise.

In praise of optimism

Types of thinking that are typical of most of us:

1. A more favourable view of our strengths and talents than is strictly merited by the past
2. An exaggerated feeling of mastery and control over events
3. An over-optimistic view of the future.

These are seen as positive enduring illusions which are beneficial in multiple ways, making us happier, more contented, more caring, and more productive and creative.

We gather information about ourselves and the world in a very incomplete way, taking shortcuts and making errors. And yet the strategy seems to work. People who are more optimistic make better choices.

Summary

All six authors of the books discussed in this chapter have emphasised spirituality of some kind as a key factor in a fulfilled life. Seligman and Gaffney have identified spirituality as **the** key factor in flourishing. Such is the scope of these studies, that, taking them all together they constitute a consensus account of the global conditions necessary for authentic human well-being. They are an extensive fleshing out of the Universal Declaration of Human Rights. How many would have thought four decades ago that this would come to pass.

Since my book is about spirituality, I have dealt mainly with those sections of the six books which emphasis spirituality. Only by reading the actual books can one appreciate fully their overall approach to human well-being. All six authors, as well as being renowned theorists, have decades of experience in their fields. All endorse the bottom-up approach as crucial for successful implementation

In addition to the theory and practice of flourishing, Maureen Gaffney's book contains relevant up-to-date information on the latest research findings in psychology. So too does her popular TV course on flourishing, which goes a long way towards a course in cognitive behaviour therapy that could make normally well people even better.

CONCLUSIONS

The Objectives of This Book

The main objectives of this book have been:

1.   To strengthen and inspire spirituality in its readers.

Most of them will have read some spiritual books, practice daily creativity in their human interactions, and contribute to charities both at home and abroad. I believe that it will also strengthen everyone's spirituality to be aware of the growing world-wide agreement that a good life must put spirituality at the top of its agenda. For that reason the book gives a chapter to secular human development movements, and describes the movement towards securing an overlapping consensus in pluralist societies.

The strong counter-forces have been mentioned. Readers will already have been well aware of them. The book also shows, however, that business organisations which would have seen themselves as counter-forces a few decades ago have joined the spirituality campaign. The Flourishing Movement is an excellent example.

2.   To make readers aware of how the new scientific vistas can enrich their personal spiritualities.

3.   To present clear evidence of the Afterworld.

World-wide, a clear majority of people believe in an afterlife. This holds also for the developed Western nations. The book provides overwhelming scientific evidence that an Afterworld exists where people of good will live joyful and creative lives aimed at helping those who are still alive.

4.   To present clear evidence of reincarnation.

The estimated number of properly validated cases must be seen as a minimum. They have come from specially organised centres around the globe. No estimates have been made for communities who have no such centre. Real numbers are, therefore, almost certainly much greater. A further problem is that a person may never become aware that he or she is a reincarnate.

Taking all factors into account, the reality of incarnation is beyond reasonable doubt.

5.   Another main aim of the book has been to articulate a rational and coherent spiritual cosmology which will make sense to both religiosts and naturalists in our scientific age. The book proposes that Ervin Laszlo's scientific cosmology best satisfies this requirement "as of now" (Laszlo). Religiosts will include God in their cosmology, in respectful disagreement with Naturalists.

6.   A sixth main aim of the book is simplicity in writing and and in reasoning as far as possible, given a number of complex topics. Readers will be the judge of that.

7.   A seventh main aim was to get the book into the hands of as many people as possible. This would be achieved by means of a modest selling price and an effective publicity and distribution system within the confines of the resources available.

8. Ecumenism was very much in mind throughout the book.

Dogma and Simplicity

Clear concepts about the attributes of God, and about the teaching and way of life of Jesus, are fundamental in a way that Magisterial dogmas no longer are. Pope John Paul II in leaving it to each Christian whether to believe in reincarnation or not, surely struck the right note.

There are other teachings in the Catholic Church which people take as dogmatic, even though they might not in fact be dogmas. Given the new scientific vistas it would be good if a clear list of actual dogmas was now updated.

The Bottom-up Approach in Social Change

Again and again throughout this book we have seen one great principle of establishing reforms that are lasting: *Acceptance of reforms that are lasting must come from the bottom* up. Reforms that come from the top may not take on at the bottom, and if they do, they are rarely lasting.

We have seen that in our contemporary world the *bottom-up approach* is sacred in world-wide movements that are focussed on social change.

The 2014 book *The Great Reformer*, a biography of Pope Francis by Austin Ivereigh, portrays the Pope's great belief in the faith and social solidarity of every-day people, especially the poor. Hopefully he will lead the way to the future, with appropriate strategies, timing, tactics, and pace. He has given many indications of his belief that lasting social change cannot be rushed, but that there is a way to achieve such change with gain to everyone.

Cosmic Creativity

"Love is the way to supercoherence. Achieving it is health enhancing and socially and ecologically sound. It gives rise to behaviours and aspirations that are good for us, good for others, and good for the world. Supercoherence is objectively good. It is the highest value philosophers called "The Good."".

Here I recall Ervin Laszlo's definition of the Good. That definition expresses a common goal which can inspire both religiosts and naturalists. Religiosts will retain their own additional source of inspiration, but Nature provides an enormous arena over which an overlapping consensus is possible. Here Religiosts and Naturalists can join forces.

The spiritual aspirations of Humanists are aimed at a Good similar to that defined by Laszlo. Humanists can share the same overlapping consensus and still hold to the belief that there is no Afterworld.

Clearly the governing body of Princeton University is backing Laszlo's definition of the good. (See Ch 6.)

Irish Murdoch's books, *The Sovereignty of Good* and *Metaphysics As a Guide to Morals,* cohere with *Laszlo*'s concept of the Good.

Secular Concepts of an Overlapping Consensus

The modern concept of an overlapping consensus was first promoted by the great German philosopher, Jurgen Habermas, who is an avowed naturalist. A number of other international luminaries who are naturalists have joined him in a public debate on the issue. They include Richard Rorty and others.

Members of the Catholic Hierarchy are also participating in the debate. Cardinal Ratzinger, later Pope Benedict XVI, was the instigator on the Catholic side.

Main Conclusions

Jesus is a repeat reincarnate who has reached the highest level of divinity that a human being can reach. His spiritual powers are in accordance with his level of divinity.

Taking into account everything that we now know, we can say that the probability of a World of Cosmic Consciousness (or Cosmic Awareness), as a part of Nature, is in the high range.

All the levels of Awareness above the level of our normal everyday world are extensions of the level pertaining to this everyday world. All belong within the Natural Cosmos or Nature.

The modern secular global movements whose aim is human development, have secular spiritual dimensions which converge towards supercoherence and the Good

Summary

The concept of a Cosmic Consciousness, as developed by Ervin Laszlo and his colleagues has achieved practical progress on a secular agenda. More nations around the globe, including the Far East are seeking his advice. The various secular agencies who are engaged in human development projects around the world are in increasing demand.

Looking back at the long-term evolution of human awareness, it seems remarkable that these different strands, whose origins were quite separate, have suddenly converged. It looks like the work of a meta-agency. Are we on the cusp of a second Axial Age. These convergences are providing effective ecumenism. They also seems to have the potential to secure a universal peace on our planet.

Will it succeed, or will it, like the first Axial Agenda, run into the sand and be followed by another epoch of wars? We don't know. We do know that if we don't make a really serious commitment, history will repeat itself.

Booklist A – Spiritual Readings That Most Influenced This Book - See Page xx

Book List B – *Books Relating to the Supernormal*

1) Keltner, Dacher - *Born to Be Good* – 2009
2) Fodor, Jerry A. and Piattelli-Palmarini, Massimo – *What Darwin Got Wrong*–2011
3) Grof, Stanislav – *The Cosmic Game*– 1998
4) Sheldrake, Rupert – *The Sense of Being Stared* – 2013
5) Sheldrake, Rupert – *The Presence of the Past* – 2012
6) Fox, Matthew and Sheldrake, Rupert – *The Physics of Angels* – 2014
7) Tucker, Jim B. and Stevenson, Ian – *Life Before Life* – 2005
8) Long, Jeffrey and Perry, Paul – *Evidence of the Afterlife* – 2011
9) Van Lommel, Pim – *Consciousness Beyond* – 2011
10) Beauregard, Mario – *Brain Wars* – 2002
11) Carter, Chris and Sheldrake, Rupert – *Science and Psychic Phenomena* – 2012
12) Parma, Sam – *The Lazarus Effect* – 2013
13) Laszlo, Ervin – *The Akashic Experience* – 2009
14) Laszlo, Ervin – *The Self-Actualizing* – 2014
15) Dossey, Larry – *The Power of Premonitions* – 2009
16) Radom, Dean — 2013
17) Semkiv, Walter – *Born Again* – 2013
18) Semkiv, Walter – *Origin of the Soul and the Purpose of Reincarnation* – 2012
19) Peterson, Wayne S. – *Extraordinary Times, Extraordinary People* – 2003
20) Frankiel (PhD), Tamar – *Kabbalah* – 2006
21) Churchland, Patricia S. – *Touching a Nerve* – 2013

Booklist C – *Other Recommended Books*

1) Comte Sponville, Andre - *The Little Book of Atheist Spirituality* – 2008
2) Cornell, John - *Darwin's Angel* – 2007
3) Dawkins, Richard – *The God Delusion* – 2006
4) Dennett, Daniel - *Breaking the Spell* – 2006
5) Dennett, Daniel – *Freedom Evolves* - 2003
6) Flanagan, Owen - *The Really Hard Problem* – 2007
7) Harris, Sam - *The End of Faith* – 2005
8) Hitchens, Christopher - *God Is Not Great* – 2007
9) Rorty, Richard and Vattimo, Gianni –*The Future of Religion* – 2005
10) Rorty, Richard - *Philosophy and Social Hope* - 1999
11) Ratzinger, Joseph Cardinal – *Truth and Tolerance* – 2004
12) O'Donohue, John - *Anam Cara* – 2008
13) Taylor, Charles – *Varieties in Religion Today* - 2002
14) Taylor, Charles – *The Ethics of Authenticity* – 1992
15) Taylor, Charles - *Sources of the Self* – 1989
16) Hanh, ThichNhat - *Living Buddha, Living Christ* – 1995
17) Hanh, ThichNhat - *The Heart of the Buddha's Teaching* – 1998
18) Clark, Mary E. - *In Search of Human Nature* – 2002
19) Scientific American Special Edition (*Volume 13, Issue 2 –Human Evolution*–2003
20) Fletcher, Richard - *The Conversion of Europe* – 1997
21) Kirsch, Jonathan – *God Against the Gods* – 2004
22) Lewis, Bernard - *The Crisis of Islam* – 2003
23) Murdoch, Iris - *Metaphysics as a Guide to Morals* – 1992
24) Sartre, J.P. - *Existentialism and Humanism* – 1946
25) Steiner, George - *Real presences* – 1989
26) Stepaniants, Marietta - *Introduction to Eastern Thought* – 2002
27) Tillich, Paul – *The Courage to Be* - 1952
28) Tillich, Paul – *Love, Power, and Justice* - 1954
29) Tillich, Paul - *Morality and beyond* – 1964
30) McGinn, Colin - *The Mysterious Flame* – 1999
31) McDonagh, Enda – *Faith in Fragments* – 1996
32) MacIntyre, Alasdair – *After Virtue* – 1985

33) Midgley, Mary - *The Myths We Live By* - 2003

34) Midgley, Mary – *Wickedness* – 2004

35) Seligman, Martin – *Flourish* – 2011

36) Brooks, Michael – *13 Things That Don't Make Sense* – 2009

37) Morris, Simon Conway – *Life's Solution* – 2003

38) Davies, Paul - *The Eerie Silence* – 2010

39) Greene, Brian - *The Fabric of the Cosmos* – 2004

40) Krauss, Lawrence M. - *A Universe from Nothing* – 2012

41) Wilson, Edward Osborne – *Consilience: The Unity of Knowledge* –1998

42) Wilson, Edward Osborne - *The Future of Life* – 2002

43) Wright, Robert - *The Moral Animal* – 1994

44) Donaldson, Margaret - *Human Minds: An Exploration* – 1992

45) Czikszentmihalyi, Milhaly - *Living Well* – 1997

46) Moane, Geraldine – *Gender and Colonialism* - 2011

47) Israel, Jonathan – *Radical Enlightenment* – 2002

48) Schleiermacher, Friedrich – *On Religion* – 1994

49) de Chardin, Teilhard – *Phenomenon of Man* – 2008

50) Polyani, Michael – *Personal Knowledge* – 1974

51) Voegelin, Eric - *Science, Politics and Gnosticism* – 1997

52) Buber, Martin – *I and Thou* - 1971

53) Buber, Martin - *Between Man and Man* – 2014